SHOULD CHRISTIANS SUPPORT ISRAEL?

by John Hagee

© Copyright 1987 by Dominion Publishers
All rights reserved
Printed in United States of America

TABLE OF CONTENTS

PART ONE:
THE ROOTS OF CHRISTIAN ANTI-SEMITISM!

Chapter 1
The Ghost of Hitler Lives!..1

Chapter 2
Who Are The Jews?..35

PART TWO:
CHRISTIAN MYTHS CONCERNING THE JEWS!

Chapter 3
"The Jews Are the Christ Killers!"..47

Chapter 4
"The Jews Rejected Jesus As Messiah!"..................................59

Chapter 5
"The Church Has Replaced Israel!"..73

Chapter 6
"The Jews Have No Right to the Land of Israel!"..................89

Chapter 7
"The Old Covenant is Dead!"..105

Chapter 8
The Mystery of Israel..119

PART THREE:
OUR DEBT OF GRATITUDE TO THE JEWISH PEOPLE!

Chapter 9
Just How Jewish Was Jesus?..131

Chapter 10
"And In Thee Shall All Nations Be Blessed"........................149

Chapter 11
Should Christians Support Israel?..165

DEDICATION

"He who gives a book gives more than cloth, paper, and ink—more than leather, parchment, and words. He reveals a forward of his thoughts, a dedication of his friendship, a page of his presence, a chapter of himself, and an index of his love." —Unknown

This book is lovingly dedicated to my wife,
DIANA CASTRO HAGEE

CHAPTER ONE
THE GHOST OF HITLER LIVES!

If you do not believe the Bible to be the inspired Word of God... put this book down! This is not another book of religious rhetoric telling you how to be happy without being holy, successful without sacrifice or how to conquer without conflict!
This book is a declaration of War!
It is not a war against men ... it's a war against a message which is an ancient Godless heresy that is again raging through the Church masquerading as truth. This heresy is now being presented under many names, (Kingdom Now, Kingdom Age, New Wave and New Age) but its prevailing amillenial, allegorical message is;
- The Church must know that she is the true Israel!
- The Jews do not have a claim to the land of Israel!
- Israel is not blessed above all nations!
- Israel is not reborn!
- The Jews rejected Jesus and should be punished.
- The Jews are the Christ killers, well poisoners, plague carriers, host defamers, and sons of the devil!
- The Old Covenant is Dead and replaced by the New Covenant!
- The Jews are our misfortune and have not blessed the nations of the earth!

This is the message of anti-Semitism! Webster defines "anti-Semitism" as "one who is hostile to or discrim-

2 / The Ghost of Hitler Lives!

inates against Jews." It is now being preached from Christian pulpits Sunday after Sunday, from coast to coast, to a laity that has been duped into believing the pastor or priest speaks only the truth!

The truth is not what your pastor says it is, the truth is not what your priest says it is, the truth is not what I say it is, *the truth is what God's Word says it is!* "Let God be true but every man a liar" (Romans 3:4).

This heresy of hatred is being taught in Sunday Schools to young impressionable minds that are learning to "hate thy neighbor" in the name of God. There is a generation of children growing up in America's Sunday Schools believing that the heartless Jews captured and crucified the only begotten Son of God. (This Christian myth will be scripturally destroyed later in the text).

Anti-Semitism is again being proclaimed by bellicose clerics as a Christian virtue, who claim they are "defending the faith" and "fighting the devil" when they attack the Jews.

Adolf Hitler felt the same way. He said, "I am acting in accordance with the will of the Almighty Creator: by defending myself against the Jew, I am fighting for the work of the Lord."[1]

Christian Anti-Semitism

Anti-Semitism has its origin and its complete root structure in Christianity! Until anti-Semitism is stopped in the Church, anti-Semitism will not be stopped on the face of the earth!

The Ghost of Hitler Lives! / 3

The very phrase "Christian Anti-Semitism" is an absolute contradiction in terms. Anti-Semitism is a synonym for hatred. Christian is a synonym for love. An anti-Semite is a dead Christian whose hatred has strangled his faith.

The Christian doctrine of love was first taught by a Jewish Rabbi from Nazareth saying; "Love thy neighbor as thyself" (Matthew 19:19). "Love one another as I have loved you" (John 15:12). "By this sign shall all men know that you are my disciples if you have love one to another" (John 13:35). "Love your enemies" (Matthew 5:44). St. Paul said, "Love worketh no ill toward his neighbors" (Romans 13:10).

When did this doctrine of hate toward the Jewish people begin? It did not begin with the Holocaust and Adolf Hitler who said, "I am only continuing the work of the Catholic Church."[2]

It did not begin with Martin Luther who said, "Know Christian, that next to the devil thou hast no enemy more cruel, more venomous and violent than a true Jew."[3] Luther died a vicious and bitter anti-Semite because the Jews would not accept his new brand of Christianity!

Anti-Semitism did not begin with the "Protocols of the Learned Elders of Zion," a diabolical lie contrived by the Russian Czarist Secret Police in 1905. Anti-Semitism did not begin in America when Henry Ford published those "Protocols of the Learned Elders of Zion" which many Americans believe to be an authentic document. The *Protocols* described an alleged international takeover of the nations by the Jews.

4 / *The Ghost of Hitler Lives!*

Logic demands these questions be asked: "If the Jews controlled the nations of the earth, how in the name of God did they manage to get six million of themselves killed in the Holocaust? How is it, since 70 A.D. when Titus invaded Jerusalem, the Jews have been scattered among the nations of the earth, denied legal rights, denied the right to own land, denied to practice their faith, denied their very lives by religious mad men who demanded they "convert to Christ or be killed?" Is that control?

Where are the Jews of Spain? They were murdered in cold blood by the Roman Church! Where are the Jews of Portugal? They were murdered in cold blood by the Roman Church! Where are the Jews of Italy and France? They were murdered in cold blood by the Roman Church! Where are the Jews of Austria and Hungary? A Godless theology of hate that no one dared try to stop for a thousand years, produced a harvest of horror. When the Pale Rider of Death thrust in the sickle, the rivers of Europe turned red with the blood of the Jews. *They were all killed in the name of a loving God!*

How did this anti-Semitic hatred get into the blood stream of Christianity? Men are not born with hate in their blood. This infection must be acquired by contact; it may be injected deliberately or even unconsciously, by parents, preachers or teachers. This disease may spread throughout the land like a plague, so that a class, a religion, a nation will become the object of *popular religious hatred* without anyone knowing exactly how it all began. The end result is a message of "hate thy neighbor."

Adversus Judaeos

Anti-Semitism in Christianity began with the early church fathers ... Eusebuis, Cyril, Constantine, St. John Chrysostom, Augustinus, Origen, Justin, and Jerome who published papers and pamphlets historically known as Adversus Judaeos. This stream of venom out of the mouths of spiritual leaders to virtually illiterate congregants, sitting benignly in their pews, listening to their pastors label the Jews as "the Christ killers, plague carriers, demons, children of the devil, blood thirsty pagans who look for an innocent child during the Easter week to drink his blood, money hungry Shylocks, who are as deceitful as Judas was relentless. The church fathers spelled his name "Jewdas." As Pope Gelasius I (492-496) philosophized: "In the Bible the whole is often named after the part; as Judas was called a devil and the devil's workman, he gives his name to the whole race." The church fathers did not tell you who to kill; they told you who to hate!

Every Christian of conscience must answer this question; "How did it happen that the first church, began by a Jewish Rabbi and his twelve Jewish disciples, within two hundred years of the resurrection began to kill Jews as a matter of church policy?

What happened to the family of our Lord Jesus Christ after the resurrection? What happened to his brothers and sisters that were born to Mary and Joseph? What happened to the disciples, their wives and their children and their children's children? They were all Jews!

6 / The Ghost of Hitler Lives!

When General Titus came marching from Rome in 70 A.D., the Jews were crucified on Roman crosses while their wives and children were forced to watch. This bloody demonstration of mass crucifixion was brutal proof that no one could resist mighty Rome and live!

What happened to the family of our Lord when Hadrian came from Rome in 135 A.D. to crush the Second Revolt? How dare these stubborn monotheistic Jews, loyal to the God of Abraham, refuse to bow their knees to a pagan culture that served hundreds of gods? The sons of Israel fought valiantly until one-half million perished at the point of Rome's sword!

Constantine, a Roman emperor who ruled in 306-337 A.D., "Christianized" the Roman Empire. In one day, with one swing of the pen, he made Rome's version of Christianity the official state religion. That religion was and is full of idolatry! The monotheistic Jews refused to worship statues of men, birds and animals. The words of God as given through Moses still rang in their ears, "Hear O Israel, the Lord our God, the Lord is one" (Deuteronomy 6:4). "Thou shalt have no other Gods before me" (Exodus 20:3).

The theology of the devout Jews was more than pagan Rome could understand and certainly more than it would tolerate. The Roman conclusion was; "The Jews are just stubborn, rebellious people!"

Constantine and his clergymen at the Council of Nicea quickly began enacting a series of restrictive edicts against the Jewish people. His purpose was to separate Gentiles and Jews from worshipping together.

The Ghost of Hitler Lives! / 7

In his words, he considered the Jews an "evil and preverse sect... let us have nothing to do with the Jews who are our adversaries, in order that we no more have anything in common with these parasites and murderers of our Lord."[4]

The Golden Mouth

The venom of Christian hatred for the Jews reached its crescendo with the coming of St. John Chrysostom (387-407 A.D.), a raving anti-Semite who is known historically as the "Golden Mouthed Orator." His blazing Jew hating sermons were classic Christian reading for centuries. Chrysostom ranted, "How can Christians dare 'have the slightest converse' with Jews, 'the most miserable of all men' (Homily 4:1), men who are' ... lustful, rapacious, greedy, perfidious bandits.' Are they not 'inveterate murderers, destroyers, men possessed by the devil' whom 'debauchery and drunkenness have given them the manners of the pig and the lusty goat. They know only one thing, to satisfy their gullets, get drunk, to kill and maime one another...' (1:4). Indeed 'they have surpassed the ferocity of wild beasts, for they murder their offspring and immolate them to the devil' " (1:6).

Chrysostom said of the Synagogue... "not only is it a theater and a house of prostitution, but a cavern of brigands, and a 'repair of wild beast' (6:5), 'the domicile of the devil (1:6), as is also the souls of the Jews' (1:4 & 6). Indeed Jews worship the devil; their rites are 'criminal and impure;' their religion is 'a disease' (3:1).

8 / The Ghost of Hitler Lives!

Their synagogue is 'an assembly of criminals ... a den of thieves ... a cavern of devils an abyss of perdition" (1:2 & 6:6).
Why did Chrysostom hate the Jews? "Because of their 'odious assassination of Christ' (6:4). This supreme crime lies at the roots of their degradation and woes (6:1). And for this deicide (God-killers), Chrysostom declares, there is 'no expiation possible, no indulgence, no pardon' (6:2). 'God hates the Jews and always hated the Jews' (6:4 & 1:7). 'I hate the Jews also because they outrage the law ...' " (6:6).
The words of this honored clergyman rang in the ears of Christianity for 1600 years. "God hates you ... and I hate you."
The natural progression for popular hatred is action. Religious belief fosters deep feeling, and deep feeling demands action to be taken to support that basic belief. Christian action toward the Jews exploded with a demonic violence beyond comprehension.
At Easter, when the Christian clergy would enflame the passions of the faithful with the vengeful message that "the Jews are the killers of Christ," the saints (sic) would race out of the church toward the Jewish quarter with clubs and beat Jews to death for what they did to Jesus on the cross.
It became an annual custom at Easter to drag a Jew into the church and slap him on the face before the altar. "This ceremony was sometimes carried out with excessive vigor; on one occasion, recounts a monkish chronicler (without, however, expressing any disapproval), a distinguished nobleman who was taking part

of chief celebrant 'knocked out the eyes and the brains of the perfidious one (disbelieving Jew), who fell dead on the spot... his brethren from the synagogue took the body out of the church and buried it."[6]

The Crusades

The perfection of Christian hatred gave birth to the Dark Ages and the Crusades. During the First Crusade to the Holy Land, in 1096, the Crusading armies called "Knights of the Cross" left a trail of Jewish blood across Europe. Within a three month period, 12,000 Jews were slaughtered in Germany as the Crusaders screamed "The Jews have killed our Savior. They must convert or be killed."

Some Jewish communities were given the opportunity to save their lives by meeting the Crusaders demand for huge amounts of gold and silver. Those Jewish communities who could not meet the ransom demand were butchered by the "will of God." Others ran to the synagogue, locked the doors, said a final prayer and killed their wives and children mercifully and quickly, lest the cross carrying Crusaders butcher them. The fathers committed suicide to preserve the sanctity of the name of Jehovah God.

The Crusaders were not holy men on a holy mission. They were a motley mob of thieves and robbers whose sins had been forgiven in advance by the Pope. Any man who "answered the call of the Crusade" could consider all his financial debts to any Jewish creditor canceled. It was a quick way to get out of debt. As a

10 / *The Ghost of Hitler Lives!*

bonus, the Crusaders were permitted to rob the Jews of their possessions on the road to and from Jerusalem. If they murdered the Jews, and raped their daughters and wives, all was *forgiven in advance* by the Pope before they left on the Crusade. This was done because "it was the will of God."

It is no wonder that the word "crusade" makes the Jews of the world nauseous. A Christian sees the Cross and thinks of forgiveness of a sin; a Jew looks at the Cross like an electric chair in the death house.

When the First crusade under Godfrey reached Jerusalem in 1099, the Crusaders invaded the city through the Jewish quarter. In a desperate attempt to save their lives, 969 Jewish men, women and children ran for the synagogue for protection, locking the doors behind them. The Crusaders promptly set fire to the synagogue and listened to helpless women and innocent children scream in horror, begging for mercy as they were burned alive. The Crusaders marched around the synagogue singing triumphantly, "Christ, We Adore Thee" as more than nine hundred members of the family of our Lord were cremated.

G.K. Chesterton (1874-1936), Catholic author whose works are used in parochial schools, expressed his regret "that the Crusaders who slaughtered Jewish men, women and children could not be canonized."[7]

Jesus Christ of Nazareth, a prominent New Testament Jewish Rabbi said, "Inasmuch as you have done it unto the least of these my brethren, (the Jews) you have done it unto me" (Matthew 25:40).

The Fourth Lateran Council of 1215

The Fourth Lateran Council met in November of 1215 in response to the call of Pope Innocent III. There were more than a thousand Church delegates who met in four stormy sessions to determine what the official relationship between Christians and Jews should be, as approved by the Roman Church. The official Christian policy that came out of the Fourth Lateran Council was a formal declaration supporting the conduct of the Roman Church toward the Jews for centuries prior. It would be the officially approved standard of conduct for European Christians toward Jews until Adolf Hitler came to power. The Fourth Lateran Council decided that all Jews must wear ...

The Badge of Shame

Concerned that Christians and Jews would engage in sexual intercourse, the Church fathers forced the Jews to wear distinctive clothing so that they could be recognized on sight. "That the crime of such a sinful mixture shall no longer find evasion or cover under pretext of error, we order that the Jews of both sexes, in all Christian lands and at all times, shall be publically differentiated from the rest of the population by the quality of their garment, especially since this is ordained by Moses ..."[8]

The reference to "this is ordained by Moses" refers to the fact that Moses instructed the men of Israel to make Prayer Shawls (Numbers 15:37-41) that were to

12 / *The Ghost of Hitler Lives!*

be worn by all adult men from "generation to generation." Jesus Christ wore a Prayer Shawl from his thirteenth birthday until the day of his crucifixion.

The Church fathers used Moses' description of a Prayer Shawl as scriptural justification to force all Jews of "both sexes in all Christian lands" to dress distinctively.

When Adolf Hitler came to power, he used this long established Roman Church policy to force the Jews to wear the Yellow Star of David, marking them for abuse and execution.

The Fourth Lateran Council also ruled that the Jews must ...

Tithe to the Roman Church

The Jews were ordered by the Council to pay tithes (ten percent of their gross income) to the Roman Church because the Jews were now owners of lands that had previously belonged to Christians. The Roman Church could not afford a loss of revenue just because a Christian had sold his property to a perfidious Jew. The exact reading of the Council edict states: "And under the threat of the same penalty (social and economic boycott by the church) we decree that Jews should be compelled to make good the tithes and dues owed to the churches which the churches have been accustomed to receive from the houses and other possessions of the Christians before they came into possession of the Jews, *regardless of the circumstances,* so that the church be preserved against loss." This ecclesiastical edict was nothing short of extortion. It was economic control of the Jews via law!

On April 1, 1933, sixty days after Adolf Hitler had sworn before the German people to "conduct my affairs of office impartially and with justice to everyone," declared a general boycott of every Jewish business in the Third Reich. It was economic control of the Jews through law!

Jews were ordered to paint a Yellow Star of David in the front window so that all good Germans would know to boycott that store. Signs were also hung on the stores which said in large bold letters, "Germans! Don't buy from Jews!" With the Jews now under boycott, Hitler turned his attention toward the Civil Service.

On April 7, 1933, the Third Reich passed a law with the pompous title, "Law for the Restoration of the Professional Civil Service." The lofty sounding piece of legislation was the legal instrument through which the Nazis dismissed every Jew working a civil service job in Germany. Thousands of Jews were without jobs overnight. It was economic control of the Jews through law, a long standing Roman Church policy!

The Fourth Lateran Council also decreed that *Jews could not hold public office* and called upon the secular powers to *"exterminate all heretics."*[9] When Hitler came to power he dutifully followed all four of these Roman Church policies.

The Spanish Inquisitioin

The Spanish Inquisition began in 1481, striking the Jews like a bolt of thunder out of the blue heavens.

14 / *The Ghost of Hitler Lives!*

For years the Jews of Spain were under extreme pressure to convert to the Roman Church. Many did and were called "Marranos" (Spanish word for pigs). They were hated by the Jews for being traitors to Judaism and were hated by the Roman Church who believed these "converts" were practicing Judaism secretly while pretending to be good Catholics.

All attempts to separate the new converts from Judaism via legislation, ghettoization or education were fruitless. From the second half of the 15th century, public discussions were conducted to determine what to do about this religious and social problem.

In 1474, when Ferdinand and Isabella ascended to the throne of Castile, the opportunity for a radical solution was at hand. They could not have consolidated their political rule without the assistance of the Church. In exchange for the support of the Church, Ferdinand and Isabella introduced a series of restrictive orders against the Jews.

Religious fervor mounted until Ferdinand and Isabella appealed to Pope Sixtus IV in 1477 to establish an Inquisition. The point must be made that this Inquisition was established by the Roman Church and received its power directly from the Pope. Its purpose was to purge the Church of Jews whose conversions were in question.

Two Dominican monks, Miguel de Morillo and Juan de San Martin were appointed to lead the Inquisition on September 27, 1480. They demanded that all Judaizers who had fled the country in terror be delivered into their hands for trial. The wealthy and

The Ghost of Hitler Lives! / 15

notable personalities of the Jewish community were brought before the religious court where hundreds were burned alive at the stake and thousands returned to the church in terrified obedience.

The Inquisition was extended in October, 1483 and under the fanatical leadership of Tomas de Torquemada reached levels of torture the Jews would not experience again until Hitler's sadistic Nazi SS Corps blossomed into its highest level of madness. Pulitzer Prize winning historian, John Toland, records that, "the black clad Nazi SS was purposely constructed by Himmler, born and bred a Catholic, on Jesuit principles by assiduously copying the service statutes and spiritual exercises presented by Ignatius Loyola." (John Toland "Adolf Hitler" Vol. 2, pg. 869)

In the fanatical effort to determine who was truly a loyal Catholic and who was not, Jewish children were choked to death in the presence of their parents. The naked breast of women were shriveled with hot irons to make them betray their husbands. The bodies of the husbands were stretched on the rack where they were pulled in half forcing them through excruciating pain to denounce their wives and children as false converts.

A major emphasis of the Inquisition was to steal the wealth of the Jews for the benefit of the royal court and the Roman Church. The faithful became so enthusiastic in the expropriating of Jewish wealth and property that the bones of dead Jews were dug up for "trial" so estates could be confiscated from their heirs.

Manuals of the Inquisition were published which gave hints on how to spot a "backsliding" Jew and how

16 / The Ghost of Hitler Lives!

to extend and intensify the suffering of the Jewish subject by flame, garrote, rack, whip or needle. This cruelty, in the name of Christ, reached an art that left Heydrich and Eichmann little to add for the Third Reich.

Historian Dagobert Runes writes, "Neither illness nor pregnancy could spare a woman from the bite of the Inquisition instruments wielded by the protectors of the loving Christ. Since all the property of the convicted fell to the Inquisition corporation, to be shared equally by their majesties, there was an added incentive to intensify the Inquisition. Denouncers were well rewarded, and a person denounced was a person indicted and convicted, since no living creature could withstand the refined methods of punishment the clerics had devised. Every single part of the human anatomy had been carefully studied and experimented upon to find those most sensitive to pain."[10]

The Spanish Inquisition gave birth to the phrase "limpieza de sangre" (meaning purity of blood). The purity of blood was the major consideration in the racial background of the accused Jew. Those who could not prove beyond a shadow of a doubt that they had blood-pure Christian descent for three generations were doomed to a death of unspeakable horror.

It is to be noted that Hitler's blood-purity rule in which Germans had to prove they had no Jewish blood for three generations was clearly formulated by the Roman Church in Spain five hundred years before Hitler came to power.

The Ghost of Hitler Lives! / 17

Martin Luther

"The worse evil genius of Germany," wrote Dean Inge, "is not Hitler, or Bismarck, or Frederick the Great, but Martin Luther." Luther's hatred for the Jews "was intensified by his intellectual vanity and the vigor of his faith, which, like that of many others before and since his time, was united to an equally unshakable conviction that anyone who did not agree with him was an obstinate enemy of the Holy Spirit who deliberately closed his eyes to the truth."[11]

Martin Luther had just introduced the Reformation and was convinced that the Jewish people would be delighted with his new brand of Christianity and would join him in his assault on the Roman Church. He was wrong! In the beginning, Luther made complimentary remarks about the Jewish contribution to Christianity. When they did not join him, he turned on them with a vulgarity and vengance that greatly appealed to the German people.

Luther said of the Jews, "All the blood kindred of Christ burn in Hell, and they are rightly served, even according to their own words they spoke to Pilate."[12]

His doctrine provided many suitable texts for Hitler's program of extermination. "Verily a hopeless, wicked, venomous and devilish thing is the existence of these Jews, who for fourteen hundred years have been, and still are, our pest, torment and misfortune. They are just devils and nothing more.

"The only Bible you have any right to, he told the Jews, is that concealed beneath the sow's tail; the

18 / *The Ghost of Hitler Lives!*

letters that drop from it you are free to eat and drink."[13] This was Luther's crude description of the Jewish people eating the waste and urine of swine.

The most vicious, Jew hating statements Luther ever made were to be found in his tract entitled "Concerning the Jews and Their Lies." Luther's tract reads as follows;

"Let me give you my honest advice.

First, their synagogues or churches should be set on fire, and whatever does not burn up should be covered or spread over with dirt so that no one may ever be able to see a cinder or stone of it. And this ought to be done for the honor of God and of Christianity in order that God may see that we are Christians ...

Secondly, their homes should be broken down and destroyed. Thirdly, they should be deprived of their prayer books and Talmuds in which such idolatry, lies, cursing and blasphemy are taught.

Fourthly, their Rabbis must be forbidden under the threat of death to teach any more ...

Fifthly, passport and traveling privileges should be absolutely forbidden the Jews. Let them stay at home.

Sixthly, they ought to be stopped from usury. For this reason, as said before, everything they possess they stole and robbed from us through their usury, for they have no other means of support.

Seventhly, let the young and strong Jews and Jewesses be given the flail, the ax, the hoe, the spade, the distaff, and spindle, and let them earn their bread by the sweat of their noses as is enjoined upon Adam's

The Ghost of Hitler Lives! / 19

children. We ought to drive the lazy bones out of our system.

If, however, we are afraid that they might harm us personally, or our wives, children, servants, cattle, etc., then let us apply the same cleverness (expulsion) as the other nations, such as France, Spain, Bohemia, etc., and settle with them for that which they have extorted from us, and after having it divided up fairly let us drive them out of the country for all time.

To sum up, dear princes and nobles who have Jews in your domains, if this advice of mine does not suit you, then find a better one so that you and we may all be free from this insufferable devilish burden—the Jews."[14]

Two days later Martin Luther died!

When the Nazis placed the Jews in ghetto stables and camps, they only followed Luther's precept; when they burned Jewish synagogues, homes and schools, they only carried out Luther's will; when the Germans robbed the Jews of their possessions, they only did Luther's bidding; when the Germans reduced the Jews to concentration camp slavery, they merely followed the teaching of Luther: Make the Hebrews slaves of the serfs!

Adolf Hitler loved Luther's theology. His Nazi murder machine showed "a proper appreciation of the continuity of their history when they declared that the first large-scale Nazi program (violent physical persecution of Jews), in November, 1938, was a pious operation performed in honor of the anniversary of Luther's birthday."[15]

Adolf Hitler

Adolf Hitler's atrocities toward the Jews have been chronicled by the world's finest scholars. There is no purpose in retracing his bloody steps that dragged Europe and the world into the bowels of Hell for twelve years of an unspeakable nightmare. What is pertinent to this text is to demonstrate how that *Roman Church policy shaped the policy of the Third Reich.* When Hitler signed the Concordant with the Roman Church he said, "I am only continuing the work of the Catholic Church."[16] Let's examine the historical record of Church Policy and Nazi Policy which is taken in part from J. E. Scherer, Die Rechtsverhaltnisse der Juden in der deutsch-osterreichischen Landern (Leipzig 1901), pp 39-49.

ROMAN CHURCH POLICY	NAZI POLICY
1. Prohibition of intermarriage and of sexual intercourse between Christians and Jews, Synod of Elvira, 306 A.D.	1. Law for the Protection of German Blood and Honor, Sept. 15, 1935 (RGB1 I, 1146)
2. Jews and Christians not permitted to eat together, Synod of Elvira, 306 A.D.	2. Jews barred from dining cars, Dec. 30, 1939, Document NG-3995
3. Jews not allowed to hold public office, Synod of Clermont, 535 A.D. Also 4th Lateran Council, 1215.	3. Law for Re-Establishment of the Professional Civil Service, April 7, 1935 (RGB1 I, 175) in which Jews were expelled from office and their civil service jobs.

The Ghost of Hitler Lives! / 21

4. Jews not allowed to employ Christian servants or possess Christian slaves, 3rd Synod of Orleans, 538.

5. Jews not permitted to show themselves in the streets during Passion Week, 3rd Synod of Orleans 538 A.D.

6. Burning of the Talmud and other books, 12th Synod of Toledo, 681.

7. Christians not permitted to patronize Jewish doctors, Trulanic Synod, 692 A.D.

8. Jews obligated to pay taxes for support of the Church to the same extent as Christians Fourth Lateran Council.

9. Jews not permitted to be plaintiffs or witnesses against Christians in the Courts, 3rd Lateran Council, 1179, Canon 26.

10. Jews not permitted to withhold inheritance from descendants who had accepted Christianity 3rd Lateran Council, 1179, Canon 26.

4. Law for the Protection of German Blood and Honor Sept. 15, 1935 (RGB1 I, 1146) forbade Germans from hiring Jews.

5. Decree authorizing local authorities to bar Jews from the streets on certain days (i.e., Nazi holidays), Dec. 3, 1938 (RGB1 I, 1676).

6. Nazi book burnings in Germany.

7. Decree of July 25, 1938 (RGB1 I, 969) forbidding Germans from patronizing Jewish doctors.

8. Jews to pay a special tax in lieu of donations for Party purposes imposed on Nazis Dec. 24, 1940 (RGB1 I, 1666)

9. Jews not permitted to institute civil suits (Sept. 9, 1942 NG-151).

10. Decree empowering the Justice Ministry to void wills offending the "sound judgement of the people." July 31, 1938 (RGB1 I, 937).

22 / *The Ghost of Hitler Lives!*

11. The marking of Jewish clothes with a badge, 4th Lateran Council 1215, Canon 68.

12. Construction of new synagogues prohibited, Council of Oxford 1222 A.D.

13. Christians not permitted to attend Jewish ceremonies, Synod of Vienna, 1267 A.D.

14. Jews forced to live in ghettos away from Christians, Synod of Breslau, 1267 A.D.

15. Jews not permitted to obtain academic degrees, Council of Basel, 1434, Sessio XIX

16. Mass extermination of the Jews in the Crusades. Fourth Lateran Council called upon secular powers to "exterminate all heretics," 1215 A.D. The Inquisitions burned them at the stake by the thousands while confiscating their property.

11. Decree of Sept. 1, 1941 forcing all Jews to wear the Yellow Star of David (RGB1 I, 547).

12. Destruction of synagogues in entire Reich, Nov. 10, 1938 (Heydrich to Goring PS-3058).

13. Friendly relations with Jews prohibited, Oct. 24, 1941 (Gestapo directive, L-15).

14. Jews forced to live in ghettos. Order of Heydrich, Sept. 21, 1939 (PS-3363).

15. All Jews expelled from schools and universities throughout the Third Reich with the Law against Overcrowding of German schools and Universities, April 25, 1933 (RGB1 I, 225).

16. Hitler's "Final Solution" called for the systematic slaughter of every Jew in Europe. He took their homes, their jobs, their possessions (even their gold filled teeth), their names and finally their very lives. His justification? "It's the will of God" and "it's the work of the Church."

The Ghost of Hitler Lives! / 23

The Holocaust did not begin with Hitler lining the Jews up for the gas chamber. It began with religious leaders sowing the seeds of hatred within their congregations toward the Jewish people. Hitler quoted the Bible, chapter and verse, to justify his attack upon the Jews. It requires no genius to find a "proof-text" for hatred in the name of God. It's been done for centuries ... and it's happening again!

"In our own day, and within our own civilization," writes Dr. James Parkes, "more than six million deliberate murders are the consequence of the teachings about the Jews for which the Christian Church is ultimately responsible, and of an attitude to Judaism which is not only maintained by all the Christian Churches, but has its ultimate resting place in the teaching of the New Testament itself."[17]

"I am convinced," wrote Pierre van Passen, "that Hitler neither could nor would have done to the Jewish people what he has done ... if we had not actively prepared the way for him by our own unfriendly attitude to the Jews, by our selfishness and by the anti-Semite teaching in our churches and schools."[18]

When a German General was asked at the Nuremerg Trials for Major War Criminals how six million people could by systematically murdered by a German people who were among the world's most advanced societies, he said, "I am of the opinion that when for years, for decades, the doctrine is preached that Jews are not even human, such an outcome is inevitable."[19]

Christians have difficulty understanding why Jewish people think of Adolf Hitler as a Christian. The

24 / *The Ghost of Hitler Lives!*

Jews think Adolf Hitler was a Christian for the same reason the Southern Baptists think Billy Graham is a Christian. Billy Graham attended and graduated from a Christian school and gives dynamic public testimony that he is a Christian in good standing with the Southern Baptist Convention. When Billy Graham preaches in the Rose Bowl, he quotes the Bible and announces that he is called of God to carry out his mission. Billy Graham's life and ministry verify he is a man of God.

Adolf Hitler also attended a Christian school under the tutelage of Padre Bernard Groner. Hitler told a friend that as a small boy, it was his ardent desire to become a priest. After he had written Mein Kampf, a text of his political and personal philosophy including his desire to exterminate the Jews, he gave public testimony that "I am now as before a Catholic and will always remain so."[20]

He gave his testimony in December of 1941 when he announced his decision to implement the "Final Solution" after the bombing of Pearl Harbor. He ordered that the "killings should be done as humanely as possible. This was in line with his conviction that he was observing God's injunction to cleanse the world of vermin. He carried within him the Catholic teaching that the Jew was the killer of God. The extermination, therefore, could be carried out without a twinge of conscience since he was merely acting as the avenging hand of God."[21]

The Jewish people consider Hitler a Christian because the princes of the church scrambled to secure

The Ghost of Hitler Lives! / 25

his favor. " 'Hitler knows how to guide the ship,' announced Monsignor Ludwig Kaas." 'Even before he was Chancellor, I met him frequently and was greatly impressed by his clear thinking, by his way of facing realities while *upholding his ideals, which are noble* ... It matters little who rules so long as order is maintained.'

The Vatican was so appreciative of being recognized as a full partner that it asked God to bless the Reich. On a more practical level, it ordered German Bishops to swear allegiance to the Nationalist Socialist regime. The new oath concluded with the significant words: 'In the performance of my spiritual office and in my solicitude for the welfare and interest of the German Reich, I will endeavor to avoid all detrimental acts that might endanger it."[22]

The Jewish people consider Hitler a Christian because the Roman Church honored Hitler on his fiftieth birthday. Special votive masses were celebrated in every German church "to implore God's blessing upon the Fuhrer and the people. The Pope did not fail to send congratulations."[23]

When Hitler's blitzkrieg invaded Austria he was met by Cardinal Innitzer who "greeted him with the sign of the cross and gave assurance that so long as the Church retained its liberties, Austrian Catholics would become *'the truest sons of the great Reich* into whose arms they had been brought back on this momentous day."[24]

The Jewish people consider Adolf Hitler a Christian because when he narrowly escaped the assassination plot by his officers, Pope Pius XII sent his personal

26 / *The Ghost of Hitler Lives!*

congratulations. The Catholic press throughout the Reich piously declared "that it was the miraculous working of Providence which had protected the Fuhrer."²⁵

When Hitler's War machine crushed the brave but ill prepared Polish Army, Nazi press carried a photo of the debris with the scripture beneath: "The Lord defeated them with horse, horsemen and chariot."²⁶ When Hitler gave speeches in public, he was anointed with a supernatural demonic spirit in which he quoted sacred scripture to justify his messianic mission to purge Germany and Europe of the Jews "once and for all." His mesmerizing voice would thunder over the heads of his electrified audience, "I'm doing the will of God."

After more than forty years following the Allies liberation of the Jews from the living Hell of Auschwitz, not one word of official condemnation or excommunication has been expressed by the Vatican concerning Hitler. Why? The simple fact of history is that six million people were systematically murdered in our generation by baptized Christians in good standing with the Church.

During our generation, one third of the Jews of Europe were choked to death on Zyclon B gas, as one thousand years of Christian anti-semitism came into full bloom. When Adolf Hitler signed the Concordant of Collaboration with the Vatican on July 20, 1933 he said, "I am only continuing the work of the Catholic Church: to isolate the Jews and fight their influence." Hitler described the Concordant as an "unrestricted acceptance of National Socialism by the Vatican."

The Ghost of Hitler Lives! / 27

Hitler was not wrong! Under the terms of the Concordant, Hitler's portrait was hung in a place of respect in every Catholic parochial and Sunday school room, the bells of the church rang in celebration on each of his birthdays, as they rang throughout Germany whenever the last Jew was deported to a horrible death in the extermination camps.

Never, after the signing of this infamous Concordant, did the Church speak one word of protest against Hitler or his barbarism. The Bishops of Austria and Germany blessed the Swastika Flags of the Third Reich and pledged their loyalty "voluntarily and without duress." The Vicar of Christ looked out his window from the Vatican and watched the Nazis drag helpless women and innocent Jewish children from their homes, load them into trucks like cattle for transport to a death of horror in the extermination camps.

What happened to those Jewish children? Here are some of the answers to this question which were given at the trial of major war criminals at Nuremberg:

"They killed them with their parents, in groups and alone. They killed them in children's homes and hospitals, burying them alive and in graves, throwing them into flames, stabbing them with bayonets, poisoning them, conducting experiments upon them, extracting their blood for the use of the German army, throwing them into prison and Gestapo torture chambers and concentration camps where the children died from hunger, torture, and epidemic diseases." (Trial of the Major War Criminals, I, pg.50).

28 / The Ghost of Hitler Lives!

"Very frequently women would hide their children under their clothes, but of course when we found them we would send the children in to be exterminated." (Ibid I, pg. 251).

"Mothers in the throes of childbirth shared cars with those infected with tuberculosis or veneral disease. Babies, when born, were hurled out of these cars' windows." (Ibid III, p. 439).

"At that time, when the greatest number of Jews were exterminated in the gas chambers, an order was issued that the children were to be thrown into the crematory ovens, or into the crematory ditches, without previous asphyxiation with gas ... The children were thrown in alive, their cries could be heard all over the camp." (Ibid VIII pg. 318,319).

If Jesus and his twelve disciples had lived in Berlin, Germany in 1940, they would have been prodded into cattle cars at bayonet point and shipped to Auschwitz. *They were all Jews!*

Arriving at Auschwitz they would have been ushered into a gas chamber en masse to scratch and claw at the walls in terror as they frantically gasped for breath. The gas chamber was camouflaged as a shower room. It was an ordinary room, fitted with sealproof doors and windows, into which gas piping had been laid. The compressed gas containers and the regulating equipment were located outside and operated by the Nazi doctor on duty.

Jesus Christ, along with Peter, James, and John et al, would have been led into the shower on the pretext that they needed a shower after their long train ride from Berlin to Auschwitz.

The Ghost of Hitler Lives! / 29

They would have slowly choked to death on the Zyklon B gas for fifteen long minutes, still standing grotesquely erect because they were packed too tightly to fall. They would have been covered with sweat and urine. Their legs would have been covered with their feces. This Nazi "Final Solution" was being carried out by baptized Christians. Their preachers and political leaders had told them, "This is the will of God."

Next the teeth of Jesus and his disciples would have been broken out with pliers or hammers for the gold fillings; their hair cut off to make mattresses and their very flesh skinned for the Nazi lamp shades. Their remains would have been thrown into an oven and cremated with the stench belching out the massive smoke stacks covering the countryside.

At night, the skies over Auschwitz were red with the ashes of dead Jews ... the family of our Lord. Those ashes were used to make soap or fertilizer for the Third Reich. Think of it! Fertilizing your roses with the ashes of the Virgin Mary's family! Soaping your body down with the remains of the family of our Lord. Sleeping on a mattress of human hair provided by the family of St. Peter.

It makes an *entirely different story* when you see the Jewish people as the family of Jesus Christ. Hitler's propaganda machine separated Jesus from his Jewishness. In Hitler's writings, Jesus Christ was in fact the first Jew hater. "Christ was the greatest early fighter in the battle against the world enemy, the Jews," ranted Hitler.[27]

30 / *The Ghost of Hitler Lives!*

    Preachers in America are now attacking the Jews and Israel under the banner of "this is the will of God." They are desperately trying to separate Jesus Christ from his Jewishness and the Jewish people, calling the Jews "our dilemma." They are trying to pit the Church against the Chosen People by saying that the "church is the only true Israel." They are attacking the Jews as the Christ rejecting killers of God.
    Hitler knew that when his goose-stepping Nazi killers knelt to pray in St. Matthew's Cathedral, they must not see St. Matthew as Jewish. How could they possibly leave the sanctuary of worship and then savagely machine gun naked Jews into an open blood filled ditch if the Jews were seen as the family of our Lord?
    How could they kneel at the statue of the Virgin Mary, a Jewess, holding the Christ child in her arms, and then mercilessly slaughter 1.5 million innocent Jewish babies if these babies were perceived as being the descendants of Jesus Christ?
    How could Hitler's mindless monsters kiss the toe of St. Peter, a very prominent Jew in Christian theology, and then go shove the living kinsmen of our Lord into the gas chambers at Auschwitz? The Messiah of Germany made it easy by officially declaring, "Jesus is not a Jew!"
    And now in the eighties, more than forty years after the Beast of Berlin committed suicide and was burned to a char, his ghost is walking the platforms of America's churches as preachers are saying once again:

The Ghost of Hitler Lives! / 31

- The Church must know that she is the true and only Israel. Hitler said, "the first and greatest lie," that the Jews are "a religious community ... the Mosaic religion is nothing other than a doctrine for the preservation of the Jewish race."[28]
- Jesus did not identify with "the Jews." Hitler said, "Jesus was a Mischlinge (German for half-breed) who was conceived of God, had but two Jewish grandparents (Mary's parents), did not practice the Jewish religion nor did he marry a Jew."[29]
- The Jews rejected Jesus as Messiah and Christians should punish the Jews economically (by not going to Israel)[30] for rejecting the Son of God. Hitler's economic punishment of the Jews has been historically validated!
- The Old Covenant is dead and is replaced by the New Covenant. Hitler said, "the Mosaic religion is nothing other than a doctrine for the preservation of the Jewish race."
- The Jews have no claim to the land of Israel! Hitler was dead before May 15, 1948 when Israel was reborn. Had he been alive he would have agreed. His Nazi officers led the Arab attack on the Jews the day after the U.N. officially recognized the state of Israel!

A choice has to be made by every Bible believing Christian! Who are we to believe? Who are we to follow? The Word of God or these misguided messengers?

THE WORD OF GOD SAYS:

1) The Jewish people are the *apple* (pupil) of God's eye eye (Zechariah 2:8).
2) The Jewish people are loved of God *right now!* (Romans 11:1 and 11:11).
3) Of all the people on the face of the earth, God chose the Jewish people for his own *personal inheritance* (Psalm 33:12 and 78:71).
4) The Jewish people are the *Chosen People* (Deuteronomy 7:6).
5) Those who attack the Jews will come under *God's judgement* (Genesis 12:3 and Matthew 25:40-46).
6) God's covenant with the Jewish people is *everlasting and unconditional* (Psalms 89:30-37).
7) The borders of national Israel are completely *defined.* The U.N. and anti-Semites may be confused about the exact borders of the nation of Israel ... but God is not! (Genesis 15:18-21, Exodus 23:31 and Ezekiel 47:13-48:35).
8) The Jews have a *Biblical right* to the land of Israel! (Genesis 13:14-17 and Genesis 15:18 and Genesis 17:8).
9) Christians are *commanded* to "pray for the peace of Jerusalem" (Psalm 122:6) and "comfort my people" (Isa. 40:1).
10) All Israel shall be *saved* (Romans 11:25).
11) Men and Nations that *bless national Israel* will have God's blessing and favor (Genesis 12:3 and Luke 7).
12) The Jews will return to the land of Israel (Amos 9:11-15).

13) The city of Jerusalem will be returned to the Jewish people (Luke 21:24).
14) Israel is the only nation on the face of the earth that was created by a *sovereign act of God* (Genesis 15).
15) God has personally sworn *to protect Israel* (Ex. 23:27-28, Deut. 28:7, Psalms 122:4, Zech. 12:2-10, and Isa. 49:25 which says "I myself will fight against those who fight you").
16) Israel will become an *agricultural miracle* (Isa. 22:6, Isa. 41:18-19 and Amos 9:13).
17) All nations will worship the Messiah in the city of Jerusalem (Zechariah 8:2-3 and 14:6).
18) The Jewish people have the *Biblical right* to Judea and Samaria which is referred to in the media as the "West Bank." (Jer. 31:2-5, Psa. 69:35, and Jer. 33:6-12).

Who will you follow? Shall we follow the Word of God or be led like blind sheep by the ghost of Hitler? The choice is yours!

CHAPTER TWO
WHO ARE THE JEWS?

Hate can find a proof text and preach it with a vengence! The message of hatred is anointed by the Prince of Darkness. Hate is a cancer of the intellect! Hatred pollutes the mind! Violence follows hatred like fire follows intense heat. The question must be asked, "Where can Christians put their hatred for the Jews while they pray to a Jewish Jesus?"

"The Jews of St. John's Gospel"

For centuries preachers have invaded Christian pulpits, reading the thirty-two references of the Gospel of St. John and projected all the Jews of the world and for all time as being blood thirsty persons, torturers of the Savior, pitless killers, traitors even as Jew-das, money changers who desecrated the Temple, more cruel than beasts in demanding that the bones of the Christ be broken—the Jews were just nothing but sons of the Devil. It is the message of hatred! Some of the verses used are;

"*The Jews* persecuted Jesus and sought to kill him." (5:16)

"*The Jews* then murmured against Him, because He said, 'I am the bread which came down from heaven.'" (6:41)

"Jesus did not want to walk in Judea, because *the Jews* sought to kill him." (7:1)

"But now you (*the Jews*) seek to kill me..." (8:40)
"Then they (*the Jews*) picked up stones to throw at Him, but he Jesus hid Himself and went out of the temple..." (8:59)
"His parents said these things because they feared *the Jews*..." (9:22)
"Therefore they (*the Jews*) sought again to seize him, but He escaped out of their hands." (10:39)
"Jesus answered... so that I might not be delivered to *the Jews*..." (18:36)
"From then on Pilate sought to release Him, but *the Jews* cried out, saying, 'If you let this man go, you are not Caesar's friend.'" (19:12)
"Pilate said to them, 'Shall I crucify your king?' The Chief Priest answered, 'We have no king but Caesar!'" (19:15)
"... the doors were shut where the disciples were assembled, for fear of *the Jews*..." (20:19)

The Jews were all guilty?

For fifteen hundred years, the guilt of a handful of Jews who hated Jesus Christ because he disagreed with their doctrines, has been spread with a broad brush to include the Jewish people as a civilization. For centuries Christian leaders have taken the above verses and used them to justify anti-Semitism as a Christian virtue.

St. John Chrysostom, the Golden Mouth, wrote, "The Jews... erred not ignorantly but with full knowledge."[1] The theology of the Middle Ages, as expressed by St.

Who Are The Jews? / 37

Bernard, prospers in the Twentieth Century. Bernard said;

"*The Jews were all guilty*; they acted with deliberate malice; that their guilt was shared by the *whole Jewish people, for all time*, and that they, and their children's children to the last generation, were condemned to live in slavery as the servants of Christian princes."[2]

There is no difference between the popular religious hatred of the Church Fathers and the Nazi hatred for the Jews, save the clerical robes of the religious princes and the Swastika arm bands of the Third Reich. The question must be asked, "Who are the Jews in St. John's gospel?"

Let's compare the styles of St. Matthew and St. John in the reporting of a similiar incident and comprehend the importance of John's using the phrase "the Jews" as opposed to St. Matthew's exact identification of the participants as "Pharisees".

St. Matthew says that when Jesus healed the man with the withered hand on the Sabbath, "*the Pharisees* made a consultation how they might destroy him" (Matthew 12:14).

St. John, reporting a similiar incident, does not use the phrase "the Pharisees" but chose to use the phrase "the Jews."

"*The Jews* therefore said to him that was healed: it is not lawful for thee to take up thy bed ... therefore did the Jews persecute Jesus because he did these things on the Sabbath." (John 5:10 & 16).

"The Jews" of St. John 5:16 are "the Pharisees" of Matthew 12:14, who were constantly trying to trap Jesus in a doctrinal dispute.

When St. John describes the healing of "the man which was blind from birth" (9:1), he describes the interrogation the Pharisees forced upon the man (9:15). When the Pharisees were not satisfied with the man's response, they went to his parents to interrogate them. When the parents confessed their son had indeed been healed, but by what power they did not know, St. John says they answered in this manner, "because they feared *the Jews*" (9:22).

It is perfectly clear from the Biblical text that "the Pharisees" of 9:15 are "the Jews" of 9:22. The Pharisees represented less than one percent of the Jewish population during the ministry of Jesus Christ, while the phrase "the Jews" is taken to mean an entire civilization of people.

In this same chapter, St. John wrote that "the Jews" had agreed among themselves, if any man should confess "that he was Christ, he should be put out of the synagogue" (9:22). This agreement was reached, not by "the Jews" as a people, but by a handful of religious Pharisees that were interrogating the blind man and his parents.

Who Are The Pharisees?

Scholars estimate that there were about one million Jews in Palestine at the time of Jesus Christ. Of that one million, the Pharisees, writes Chaim Potok, "... numbered a little more than six thousand."[3] The Pharisees therefore, represented *less than one percent* of the population of Palestine.

Furthermore, the Pharisees were divided into three schools of thought. One school was led by the famous Hillel who wandered from Babylonia to Jerusalem and joined a house of study. In time, he was recognized as one of the foremost teachers of the Pharisees. He served as patriarch in Palestine from 10 B.C. until 10 A.D. and his students ruled Jewish life for more than four hundred years.

There was a second school of thought among the Pharisees under the leadership of Shammai. Shammai and Hillel agreed on nothing! They were constantly debating over who was right and who was wrong on any given scriptural issue.

There was a third school of thought represented by the Essenes that lived in the Judean desert. This is the group to which John the Baptist belonged.

The point must be made again that all three schools of the Pharisees represented less than 1% of the population of Palestine at the time of Christ.

The word "Pharisee" comes from the word "Perushim" which means to be separated. These religious separatists held themselves aloof from all other Jews and from other Pharisees that did not agree with their doctrinal teaching. They were extremely careful in matters of ritual purity and refused to touch a menstruant woman, a woman after childbirth, a corpse, a dead reptile, or a leper.

They believed that they alone were the rightful teachers and interpreters of the oral law. They believed in the resurrection of the dead, in angels and that God guided human events providentially.

Potok writes, "It is an error to see these Pharisees as gentle old men with flowing white beards; see them rather as passionate followers of scribal teachings, many adept with sword and spear as well as with text of the law, *quite willing to kill* for the sake of their God. We are talking of a time when men easily *took up the sword* for what they held dear. The Pharisees *killed for God* rather than for plunder. It is to be doubted if those who fell by Pharisee swords were thereby consoled."[4]

This is the historical setting of the Pharisees into which Jesus came and about which the Gospel of John describes. During the ministry of Jesus, there was a raging doctrinal dispute between the followers of Hillel and Shammai concerning the law of divorce. The question was, "Can a man divorce his wife for every cause?" The battle lines were drawn between the school of Shammai and the school of Hillel. This theological fight became known in history as the Shammai-Hillel dispute!

Shammai taught that a man *could not* divorce his wife "for every cause" and could only get a divorce for fornication. (Fornication in the Biblical text is a state of sin which includes adultery, homosexuality, sex with animals and lewdness). For the Jews, the scriptural right to divorce was the right to re-marry. This was accepted without question in all Israel.

Hillel was an extreme legalist who taught that a man could divorce his wife "for every cause." According to Hillel, a husband could divorce his wife for loud talk or for talking too much, for failing to prepare meals in a kosher manner, for careless seasoning of food, for going into the street with loose or uncombed hair, or if the husband found one more beautiful than his wife and many other reasons.[5]

The Hillel school of the Pharisees was constantly trying to entrap Jesus into this raging doctrinal dispute. If they could get him to commit himself and he decided not to agree with them, the religious war was on. Remember, these people killed in the name of God, anyone who disagreed with their doctrines.

The followers of Hillel approached Jesus in St. Matthew, chapter nineteen, for him to commit himself as a teacher on the "divorce for every cause" dispute.

"The Pharisees also came to Jesus, testing Him, and saying to Him, 'Is it lawful for a man to divorce his wife *for every cause?*" (Matthew 19:3)

Jesus knew his life was on the line! If he disagreed with these sword carrying legalists, they would try kill him. Jesus gave his answer, "Whosoever shall put away his wife, *except it be for fornication*, (the teaching of the school of Shammai) and shall marry another, commits adultery ..." (Matthew 19:9)

The fight was on! From that moment forward Jesus was a living devil to those Pharisees who followed Hillel. They plotted to have him killed. These were "*the Jews*" that Jesus said "were of your father the devil." These are "*the Jews*" that interrogated the parents of the blind man until they shook with fear. These are "*the Jews*" whom Jesus' disciples were hiding from behind closed doors (John 20:19).

Pharisees Loved Jesus

Many Christians fail to recognize the very obvious scriptural fact that many Pharisees were friends of Jesus. They loved him, He ate with them, they tried to save his life.

Nicodemus, a devout Pharisee, came to Jesus "by night." Entirely too much criticism has been heaped upon Nicodemus for coming to Jesus "by night" as if he were sneaking around. Nothing could be further from the truth. Nicodemus was a ruler of the Pharisees and was in the courts all day. Coming to Jesus after sundown was the only logical time to see him.

Nicodemus confessed with his mouth:

> "Rabbi, we know (the Sanhedrin knows) that thou art a teacher *come from God*: for no man can do these miracles that thou doest, except that God be with him." (St. John 3:2)

Jesus ate with the Pharisees! (Luke 7:37) In Biblical times, you did not break bread with a man unless there was a bond of mutual esteem and respect. To eat with a man and then betray him or to speak ill of him was the ultimate act of disloyalty. It was unthinkable to eat with someone and then betray him.

That's why King David said:

> "Yea, mine own familiar friend, in whom I trusted, which did eat of my bread, hath lifted up his heel against me." (Psalms 41:9)

The name "Judas" is the universal synonym for traitor. Judas betrayed Jesus Christ as they were eating the Last Supper together. It must be understood

Who Are The Jews? / 43

that Judas was not Jewish, hence the church fathers calling him "Jew-das" is in historical error.

Jesus chose the Twelve. Ten (which is a Jewish minyan) were all that was necessary for religious services to be conducted. Ten disciples were ethnic and religious Jews. Two were not ethnic Jews but were religious proselytes. They were Judas Iscariot and Simon the Canaanite.

"Judas last name was not Iscariot. Ish-Kirot means he was a foreigner, an alien to the ethnic family of Israel. "Ish" means man and "Kirot" means he was a citizen of Kir or Kirot. There was a city in southern Judea called Kirot. It was Jewish. In southern Moab, across the Dead Sea, was another Kir or Kirot.

If Judas had been from the Kirot in Judea, his name would have been Judas Mi-Kirot, as Mary from Migdol was called Mary Magdalena. Since Judas was a foreigner his name was Ish-Kirot."[6]

In the Calvary Plot that we will discuss later, we shall discover that Judas the foreigner and Herod the Idumean Jew (foreigner) had common interest in the death of Christ. Judas could have been Herod's inside man from day one in the ministry of Jesus Christ.

Why did Judas ask for thirty pieces of silver out of the non-negotiable silver sheckels of the Temple treasury? As a devout Jew he could not spend the money. As devout Jews, the Temple could not give Judas the money. Yet they did! It suggests that there was a long standing connection between Judas, Herod and his politically appointed High Priest.

"Herod will kill thee"

Further scriptural evidence that many Pharisees supported Jesus is clearly indicated in Luke 13:31; "The same day there came certain of the Pharisees, saying unto him, Get thee out, and depart hence: for Herod will kill thee."
  These Pharisees had come to warn Jesus that Herod was angry with him and would have him killed like John the Baptist. Question: If the objective *of all Pharisees* was to kill Jesus, why did these Pharisees come out to warn him?
  Everyone in Palestine knew that Herod was a cold blooded killer. If the Pharisees wanted Jesus dead, warning him was the last thing they would have done. They knew that Herod was a pathological killer who had murdered nine of his ten wives. These Pharisees came to warn Jesus in an effort to save his life because they were dear friends.

"There was division among them ..."

The division among the Pharisees about Jesus is further demonstrated in the gospel of St. John when Jesus healed the blind man by putting mud in his eyes.
  "Therefore said some of the Pharisees, This man is not of God, because He keepeth not the Sabbath day. Others said, How can a man that is a sinner do such miracles? And there *was division among them.*" (St. John 9:16)
  For eighteen hundred years, there has been no act of war against the Jews in which the Church did not

play an intrinsic part. Taking the verses of St. John's gospel to justify hatred is heresy! It's sin, and as sin, is damnable! The preacher or teacher who does so brings himself under the Genesis Curse! (Gen. 12:3)

It makes no sense to praise the dead Jews of the past (Abraham, Isaac and Jacob) while hating the Goldbergs across the street!

CHAPTER THREE
THE CHRISTIAN MYTHS CONCERNING THE JEWS!

The Word of God is not a myth! If it is, I am myth-taken, myth-tified and of all men most myth-erable. Men have taken the sacred text, twisted the truth to coincide with their prejudice, and preached it for centuries as "the gospel truth."

Again, truth is not what I say it is. Truth is not what you say it is. Truth is what God's Word says it is. Here are some Christian myths concerning the Jews that have been preached for centuries as "the gospel truth" that are in fact Christian fabrications.

Myth: "The Jews Are The Christ Killers!"

The myth began with the Church Fathers telling their illiterate congregants the Jews were the odious assassins of Christ. Century after century, the vicious label was tied about the necks of the Jews until the swords of the Crusaders, the Inquisitors and the Nazi Holocaust turned Europe red with Jewish blood because "the Jews are the Christ killers."

Eusebuis, in the first paragraph of *Church History*, declared that it was his intention to "recount the misfortunes which immediately came upon *the whole Jewish nation* in consequence of their plots against the Savior."[1]

St. Gregory of Nyssa mounted his pulpit ranting, "*slayers of the Lord,* murderers of the prophets, adversaries of God, haters of God, men who show contempt for the law, foes of grace, enemies of their fathers' faith, advocates of the devil, brood of vipers, slanderers, scoffers, men whose minds are in darkness, leaven of the Pharisees, assembly of demons, sinners, wicked men, stoners and haters of righteousness."[2]

St. John Chrysostom (345-407) who was called "the bishop with the golden mouth," was the first to use the term deicide Jews (Killers of Christ). It was a vicious label the Jews were never able to escape.

Chrysostom's anti-Semitic venom was recorded in his homilies and was classic Roman Church reading for centuries:

"The Jews are the most worthless of all men. They are lecherous, greedy, rapacious. They are perfidious *murderers of Christ.* They worship the devil, their religion is a sickness. The Jews are the *odious assassins of Christ and for killing God* there is no expiation possible, no indulgence or pardon. Christians may never cease vengence, and the Jew must live in servitude forever. God always hated the Jews. It is incumbent upon all Christians (i.e., their duty) to hate the Jews."[3]

A. Roy Eckert shows how the Nazis prepared the German people for the extermination of the Jews by exploiting this crucifixion theme with its corollary of unending divine judgement. The "Christ Killers" label motivated the German people to be silent and turn

Christian Myths Concerning The Jews! / 49

their heads while the Nazis marched the apple of God's eye toward mass extermination ditches and finally into the ovens.

One of the largest extermination pits, at Kerch, was examined in 1942 by officials in the Russian Army. This was the report:

"It was discovered that this trench, one kilometer in length, four meters wide, and two meters deep, was filled to overflowing with bodies of women, children, old men, and boys and girls in their teens. Near the trench were frozen pools of blood. Children's caps, toys, ribbons, torn off buttons, gloves, milkbottles, and rubber comforters, small shoes, galoshes, together with torn off hands and feet, and other parts of human bodies, were lying nearby. Everything was spattered with blood and brains."[4]

How could this madness happen at the hands of one of the most civilized and cultured peoples on the earth? How could it be justified in the minds of the Christian baptized German people? It was done with the oft repeated poisonous phrase; "The Jews are the Christ Killers!"

Hermann Grabe was an eye witness to what happened at Dulmo, in the Ukraine, as a result of years of religious rhetoric blaming the Jews for the crucifixion of Jesus Christ.

On October 5, 1942, Grabe went to his office in Dulmo, where he was told by his foreman that all the Jews in the neighborhood were being exterminated. About fifteen hundred were being shot each day in massive extermination ditches.

Grabe and his foreman got into a car and drove to the execution ditches the Nazis had prepared thirty meters long and three meters deep. As they arrived, they saw the Nazi SS with dog whips driving the Jews off the packed trucks toward the massive extermination ditches.

"The Jews were ordered to strip. They were told to put down their clothes in tidy order, boots and shoes, top clothing and underclothing. Already there were great piles of this clothing and a heap of eight hundred to a thousand pairs of boots and shoes.

The people undressed. The mothers undressed their little children, 'without screaming or weeping,' reported Grabe, five years after. They had reached a point of human suffering where tears no longer flow and all hope has been abandoned. 'They stood around in family groups, kissed each other, said farewells, and waited.'

They were waiting for a signal from the SS man with a whip, who was standing by the pit. They stood there waiting for a quarter of an hour, waiting for their turn to come, while on the other side of the earth mound, now that the shots were no longer heard, the dead and the dying were being packed into the pit.

Grabe said:

'I heard no complaints, no appeal for mercy. I watched a family of about eight persons, a man and a woman both about fifty, with their grown up children, about twenty to twenty four. An old woman with snow-white hair was holding a little baby in her arms, singing to it and tickling it. The baby was cooing with delight. The couple were looking at each other with tears in their eyes. The father was holding the hand of a boy about ten years old and speaking to him softly; the boy was fighting his tears ..."[5]

They were marched into the execution ditch and shot in the usual Nazi fashion in the back of the head. Dr. James Parkes writes, "In our own day ... more than six million deliberate murders are the consequences of the teachings about Jews for which the Christian Church is ultimately responsible ... which has its ultimate resting place in the teaching of the New Testament itself."[6]

One of those deadly New Testament myths is that the Jews killed Jesus! No justification can be found in the New Testament to support that myth.

In any court trial, eyewitness accounts are considered the only acceptable source of testimony in the pursuit of truth. What do the eye-witness accounts of St. Matthew, St. Mark, St. Luke and St. John have to say?

These writers took special care to impress upon their readers the fact that the Jewish people, their own people, were not responsible for, and were for the most part, ignorant of the events which led up to the apprehension, the trial and the condemnation of Jesus Christ.

St. Matthew's Eyewitness Account

St. Matthew states that "the Jews" as a people had nothing to do with the political conspiracy against

Jesus. The conspirators are exposed in chapter twenty six, verse three:
> "Then the Chief Priest and the elders of the people assembled in the palace of the high priest, whose name was Caiaphas, and *they plotted* to arrest Jesus in some sly way and to kill him." Matt. 26:3 NIV

There are two very important points that must be made here:
- There was a crucifixion plot!
- It was carried out by the High Priest Caiaphas who did not in any way represent the Jewish people as he was politically appointed by Herod who was himself directly appointed by Rome, not the Jewish people. The Jewish people hated Herod and the High Priest because they were political pawns in the hands of the pagan Romans.

How did Herod come to power? Mark Anthony of Rome joined military forces with Herod the Great, forty years before Christ was born in an attack on the city of Jerusalem. After five months, Jerusalem fell and Herod was appointed by Mark Anthony as the Roman supervisor of Palestine. He was a dictator and a paranoid murderer from whom Hitler could have learned.

Herod promptly had 45 members of the Sanhedrin Court murdered to gain absolute dictatorial control and silence the Jewish voice in government. During the reign of Herod, the Sanhedrin was nothing more than a powerless religious court. Herod now had absolute power by the will of Rome, not the Jewish people.

Christian Myths Concerning The Jews!

The High Priest, Caiaphas, who led the Calvary Plot was appointed by Herod to do the will of Rome. He was an illegitimate priest who was not selected by the Jewish people to do their will. The High Priest was a political pawn who was hated by the Jewish people!

During the Great Revolt (66-70 A.D.), Josephus records that the religious Jews burned down the house of the High Priest. Why? Because he was Rome's puppet, absolutely corrupt, whose objective was to please Rome, not the Jews of Jerusalem.

Into this political setting walks a Jewish Rabbi named Jesus of Nazareth. The Jews are looking for a Deliverer who will lead a revolt to break the oppressive chains of Rome. The popularity of Jesus spread like chained lightning. Anyone who could feed five thousand people out of one boy's sack lunch could feed an army that could defeat Rome. Anyone who could heal and raise people from the dead could heal wounded soldiers and raise dead troops back to life to fight the pagan Romans.

Jesus Christ was a very serious political threat to Herod and to his stooge High Priest, Caiaphas. So they entered into a politically inspired plot to have Jesus killed Roman style ... the crucifixion!

They Feared A Riot!

When Caiaphas, the High Priest, met with his political rogues to consider how to kill Jesus of Nazareth, the Biblical text states that they determined to arrest Jesus in a sly way lest they cause a riot among the Jewish people.

> " ... and they plotted to arrest Jesus in some sly way and kill him. But not during the Feast (Passover)," they said, "or there may be a *riot among the people.*" (Matt. 26:3 NIV)

Why did they fear a riot? A riot requires the *spontaneous uprising* among the general population! The High Priest knew that the majority of the people supported Jesus and would spontaneously riot if he were captured. News of a riot would get back to Rome, Herod would be politically embarrassed and the High Priest would be instantly replaced from his very lucrative position.

St. Matthew contributes more evidence that the leaders of this plot *feared the Jewish people* if they abused Jesus.

> "They looked for a way to arrest him, but they were *afraid of the crowd* because the people held that he was a prophet." (St. Matthew 21:46)

The High Priest and his circle of religious conspirators had no mandate from the people; rather, "they feared the people." They most certainly did not represent the one million Jews that were living in Palestine at the time, much less the millions of Jews that lived in Egypt or were scattered over the Roman Empire. These religious rogues were a miniscule handful, led by the High Priest, to do Rome's bidding.

Christian Myths Concerning The Jews! / 55

What About The Mob?

Ah yes, how many times have we heard "proof-text" Christians chatter about the mob who screamed, "His blood be upon us and upon our children," (St. Matthew 27:25) as scriptural proof that all the Jewish people on earth are forever guilty of the blood of Jesus Christ and deserve eternal punishment from the Almighty!

The scriptural fact is that the political puppet, Caiaphas, *gathered and controlled the crowd.* Remember, this is an orchestrated plot, not a spontaneous expression of the people. St. Matthew, an eyewitness, says:

> "But the chief priest and the elders *persuaded the crowd* to ask for Barabbas and to have Jesus executed." (St. Matthew 27:20)

How did they persuade the crowd? Remember those Pharisees in the school of Hillel who were mad as hornets because Jesus endorsed Shammai's teaching on "divorce for every cause?" It took no oratorical gift to get them to scream for the crucifixion of Jesus. They could not have been more than a few hundred and they were more than glad to do it.

Jesus was crucified! Big problems developed for the local theologians when on the third day he arose from the dead! The moral corruption of Caiaphas once again manifested itself. He gave large political bribes to the military guards watching the tomb and told them to lie about what had happened. Let the eye witness account of St. Matthew speak for the record:

"When the Chief Priest had met with the elders and *devised a plan*, they gave the soldiers a *large sum of money*, telling them, '*you are to say*, His disciples came during the night and stole him away while we were asleep.' If this report gets to the governor, *we will satisfy him* and keep you out of trouble. (St. Matthew 28:12-14)

There are five points that must not be missed in this important verse;

One, the Chief Priest was a conspirator!

Two, he was guilty of offering a Roman soldier a political bribe which was a criminal act punishable by death.

Three, he was a liar who paid other people to lie.

Four, the Roman soldier could have been put to death for sleeping at his post but the Chief Priest was so totally confident of his political connection to the Roman Governor, he promised to "satisfy him" and assured the soldier that he would "keep him out of trouble."

Five, the fact that the Chief Priest was politically connected was common public knowledge or else the Roman soldier would never have placed his life in jeopardy by accepting the bribe and becoming a part of this religious plot.

St. Mark's Account

St. Mark joins St. Matthew in contributing evidence that these political prostitutes did not represent the Jewish people.

Christian Myths Concerning The Jews! / 57

"The Chief Priest and the Pharisees sought how they might destroy him. For they feared him because *the whole multitude* was in admiration of his doctrine." (Mark 11:18)

"They sought to lay hands upon him, but they *feared the people.*" (Mark 12:12)

"The leaders wanted to kill him but they said, "not on the festival day, lest there be a *tumult among the people.*" (Mark 14:2)

St. Luke's Account

Permit St. Luke to join the parade of Bible witnesses by saying,

"And the Chief Priest ... sought to destroy him. And they found not what to do with him, for all the people were *very attentive to hear him.* (Luke 19:47-48)

"The Chief Priest and the Scribes sought to lay hands on him ... but *they feared the people.*" (Luke 20:19)

"And the Chief Priest and the Scribes sought how they might put Jesus to death; but *they feared the people.*" (Luke 22:2)

Jesus himself identifies His killers, "Then He took the twelve aside and said to them, 'Behold, we are going up to Jerusalem, and all things that are written by the prophets concerning the Son of Man will be accomplished. 'For He will be *delivered to the Gentiles* (the Romans) and will be mocked and insulted and spit upon. And they will scourge Him and *put Him to death.* And the third day He will rise again.'" (Luke 18:31-33)

The Bibical text is perfectly clear! Jesus was crucified by Rome as a political insurrectionist considered too dangerous to live. He was a threat to Herod's grip on Palestine! He was a threat to the High Priest! The Calvary Plot among Herod's inner circle produced the Roman crucifixion of Jesus at Calvary! It had nothing to do with the Jewish people as a civilization.

The historical fact is that three out of four Jews did not live in Palestine when Jesus began His Ministry. Nine out of ten of the Jews in Palestine during His ministry lived outside of Jerusalem. Only a few hundred of the irate Pharisees could have possibly participated in the Calvary Plot led by the High Priest.

The justice of God would never permit judgement for the sins of a handful of people to be passed to a civilization of people. In the last breath of his earthly life, Jesus forgave even the High Priest and his conspirators with "Father forgive them for they do not know what they do." (Luke 23:34)

If God has forgiven ... why can't Christianity?

CHAPTER FOUR
MYTH: THE JEWS REJECTED JESUS AS MESSIAH!

Most evangelicals believe the Jews rejected Jesus as Messiah and therefore qualify for God's eternal judgement. Replacement theologians write; "The covenant with Israel was broken because she *would not accept Jesus Christ whom God sent.*"[1]

Is that Biblically true?

There are several questions that must be answered:

- Did the Jews reject Jesus as Messiah or did Jesus refuse to be their Messiah? It can't be both ways!
- Did the words of Jesus or His actions convey the message that he wanted to be Messiah?
- Did the Jews want Jesus to be their Messiah?
- What does the Biblical text plainly state was the sovereign plan of God for the life of Jesus Christ?

God's Sovereign Will for Jesus

Anyone who reads the Bible knows that Almighty God has a sovereign will that no man or nation can change nor control. That is also true about the life of

Jesus Christ. What was God's sovereign will for his life as written in the scripture?

The Holy Spirit spoke through Simeon concerning God's sovereign will for the life of Jesus in the gospel of St. Luke.

> "So he (Simeon) came by the Spirit into the temple. And when the parents brought in the child Jesus, to do for him according to the custom of the law (circumcision), he took Him up in his arms, and blessed God, and said: 'Lord, now you are letting your servant depart in peace, According to Your word; For mine eyes have seen your salvation which You have prepared before the face of all peoples, *A light to bring revelation to the Gentiles*, and the glory of your people Israel."

God, the Holy Spirit, announced through a Jewish prophet, Simeon, that the sovereign purpose for Jesus life was for him to be a "*light to the Gentiles*" (compare Isa. 42:6).

This was a shocking revelation because the Jews considered the Gentiles unclean, they were "aliens from the commonwealth of Israel, and strangers from the covenants of promise, having no hope and without God in the world" (Ephesians 12:12).

The prejudice of the disciples against the "unclean" polytheistic Gentiles was so strong, it took a divine rebuke from the angel of the Lord to get Peter to share the gospel with the Gentiles in the home of Cornelius (Acts 10:19). When Peter saw the sheet (which was actually a Prayer Shawl) let down from heaven by its four corners and saw it full of "unclean creatures," he was

Myth: The Jews Rejected Jesus As Messiah! / 61

repulsed. That's why the Great Commission commanded "Go ye (Jews) into all the world and preach the gospel to *every creature* ... " Gentiles were considered creatures. Jesus referred to the gentiles as dogs! The message of the gospel was *from* Israel, not *to* Israel! When Peter obeyed the Lord and went to the house of Cornelius, the Jewish church was enraged that he would do such an unthinkable thing. (Acts 15; Galatians 2)

John The Baptist Speaks!

John the Baptist said to his listeners as Jesus came to the Jordan River to be baptized, "Behold the *lamb of God* which taketh away the sin of the world" (St. John 1:29).

Every Jewish person who heard John's words knew there was only one thing you could do with a young, male lamb ... kill it! John the Baptist was stating that the primary purpose for Jesus' life was the Cross ... not a crown. He spoke of Jesus death ... not His diadem.

John the Revelator joins the parade of witnesses by describing Jesus as "the Lamb slain from the foundation of the world" (Revelation 13:8). It means that it was God's sovereign will for Jesus to die from the very dawning of time. Had Jesus permitted himself to become the reigning Messiah to the Jews, he would have missed the sovereign will of God for His life.

The Crisis Theory

Replacement Theologians have created the crisis theory. It's the Catch 22 of the New Testament. The crisis theory goes like this ... "God had Plan A and

62 / Myth: The Jews Rejected Jesus As Messiah!

Plan B for the ministry of Jesus Christ while he was on earth. Plan A was for Jesus to be the Messiah of Israel. Plan B was the Cross of Calvary. Since the Jews rejected Jesus as Messiah, God had no choice but to go to Plan B ... the crucifixion."

This is utter rubbish! Firstly, it makes a sovereign and almighty God subject to the whims and choices of man.

Secondly, the Biblical text parades three witness before us (Simeon, John the Baptist and John the Revelator) who plainly state that God's plan from the beginning was for Jesus to die. Had Jesus not gone to the cross, not one Gentile would have ever come to redemption.

Jesus, "I've Come To Die!"

When Jesus spoke to Nicodemus he said, "And as Moses lifted up the serpent in the wilderness, even so must the Son of man be lifted up" (John 3:14). This is a clear reference to his death on the Cross.

When Mary of Bethany came and annointed the feet of Jesus, he said, "she is come aforehand to anoint my body to the burying" (Mark 14:8). Jesus told his disciples "Thus it is written, and thus it was necessary for the Christ to suffer and rise *from the dead* the third day" (Luke 24:46). It is obvious from the Biblical text that God's will for Jesus was to die on the Cross and that Jesus carried out that assignment with joy (Hebrews 12:2).

Myth: The Jews Rejected Jesus As Messiah!

Five major points must now be made which are crucial to understanding why the Jews did not reject Jesus as Messiah.
1) Jesus had to live to be the Messiah!
2) If it was God's will for Jesus to die from the beginning,
3) If it was Jesus intention to be obedient unto death,
4) If there is not one verse of scripture in the New Testament that says Jesus came to be the Messiah, and
5) If Jesus refused by His words or actions to claim to be the Messiah to the Jews, then *HOW CAN THE JEWS BE BLAMED FOR REJECTING WHAT WAS NEVER OFFERED?*

"Give Us A Sign!"

The Jews were accustomed to their leaders demonstrating their call from God with supernatural signs. When God called Moses from the backside of the desert to go into Egypt and lead millions of Hebrew slaves out of bondage, God gave Moses four signs to convince the Children of Israel that he was their Messiah. (It must be understood that "Messiah" in the Jewish sense means the anointed one. Every king and priest in Israel was an "anointed one.")

The first sign that God gave to Moses was for Moses himself to verify that he was indeed God's anointed. God commanded Moses to throw his shepherd's rod down on the ground and it became a snake, causing

Moses to flee from it. Any nagging doubts Moses might have had vanished! He knew he was anointed of God to overthrow Egypt and lead the Jewish people to the Promised Land.

The next two signs God gave Moses were to convince the Children of Israel that Moses was their Messiah. God told Moses to put his hand in his bosom. He did and it instantly became white with leprosy. God ordered Moses to put his hand in his bosom a second time. He did and his hand was restored "as his other flesh" (Exodus 4:7).

God continues His instructions to Moses by saying ... "if they will not believe thee, neither hearken to the voice of the first sign, that they will believe the voice of the *latter sign*" (Exodus 4:8). The Jews had been in slavery more than 400 years and it was imperative to the sovereign plan of God that the Jews recognize Moses as their Messiah.

For this reason God gave Moses a fourth sign that would convince the most skeptical Jewish slave in Egypt. God said to Moses,

> "And it shall come to pass, if they will not believe also these two signs, neither hearken unto my voice, that thou shall take the water of the river, and pour it upon the dry land: and the water which thou takest out of the river shall become blood upon the dry land." (Exodus 4:9)

Moses used these four signs to convince the Children of Israel, who had been in slavery for 400 years, that he was God's anointed leader or Messiah.

Myth: The Jews Rejected Jesus As Messiah! / 65

If God intended for Jesus to be the Messiah of Israel, why didn't He authorize Jesus to use supernatural signs to prove He was God's Messiah, just as Moses had done? The Jews, knowing of Moses signs to Israel, asked for a supernatural sign that He was indeed their Messiah. Jesus answered,

"... there shall be no sign given, except the sign of the prophet Jonah. For as Jonah was three days and three nights in the belly of the great fish, so will the Son of Man be three days and three nights in the heart of the earth" (St. Matthew 12:39-40).

Jesus refused to give a sign! He only compared himself to the prophet Jonah who carried the message of repentence from God to the Gentiles at Ninevah. Jesus was again saying, "I have come to carry a message from God to the Gentiles and will be in my grave for three days and nights as Jonah was in the whale's belly for three days and nights."

Jesus gave Peter a commission to the Gentiles with the words "Blessed art thou Simon son of Jonah" (Matthew 16:17). He was not referring to Simon's father but to the prophet Jonah, who as a Jew, reluctantly carried God's message to the Ninevites who were Gentiles.

Peter was the Jewish messenger who would, as Jonah, carry the gospel message to the Gentiles in the house of Cornelius. When the angel of the Lord found Peter, he was in Joppa on the rooftop ... the same city where Jonah had fled to avoid going to Ninevah. Both men went from Joppa to the Gentiles, both men were forced of God to go, both were extremely successful and both were rebuked by fellow Jews for going to the gentiles.

66 / *Myth: The Jews Rejected Jesus As Messiah!*

Herod Asked For A Sign!

When Jesus went on trial, Herod "was desirous to see him for a long season ... and he hoped to have seen some miracle (sign) done by him" (St. Luke 23:8). Jesus refused to produce a sign for the national leadership of Israel in an attempt to prove he was the Messiah because it was not the Father's will nor His to be Messiah. Jesus' repeated response to the Jewish people who urged him to be their Messiah was "My kingdom is not of this earth" (St. John 18:36).

"Tell No Man!"

If Jesus wanted to be Messiah why did he repeatedly tell his disciples and followers to "tell no man" about his supernatural accomplishments? Think about it! If the man were trying to gain national attention to rally the support of the general public for the overthrow of mighty Rome, he would not go around the country saying "Tell no man!"

He would have conducted himself like any other politician who would do anything the mind of man could imagine to make the CBS evening newscast with Dan Rather. The name of the game is to create public awareness. Let people know who you are and what you propose to do.

What did Jesus do?

There are sixty-four occasions in the four gospels where Jesus threw a wet blanket over his popularity, instructing those who were excited about His being

Myth: The Jews Rejected Jesus As Messiah! / 67

Messiah to "tell no man." The people wanted him to be their Messiah, but He absolutely refused.

When Jesus healed the leper, He instructed him, "See thou tell no man!" (Matthew 8:1) When He cast evil spirits out of the multitudes that followed him and they cried out saying, "Thou art the Son of God," Jesus commanded them, "that they should not make him known." When He raised Jairus' daughter from the dead, He charged the parents of the dead girl, "that they should tell no man what was done" (Luke 8:56). When He opened deaf ears, "He charged them that they should tell no man" (Mark 7:36). When He healed the blind man at Bethsaida by spitting on his eye, He ordered him, saying, "Neither go into the town, nor tell it to anyone in the town" (Mark 8:26). When Jesus healed two blind men at once in Matthew chapter nine, He "charged them straightly, saying, 'See that no man know it" (Matthew 9:30).

When impetuous Peter could stand it no longer, he blurted out, "Thou art the Christ." You are the anointed one! You are the Messiah that will lead the Jews in their revolt against Rome. Jesus commanded His disciples, "that they should tell no man of him" (Mark 8:30).

After the transfiguration where the disciples had heard Moses talking to Jesus and the voice of God spoke from the cloud saying, "This is my beloved Son: hear him," Jesus commanded His disciples as they were coming down the mountain to "tell no man what they had seen, till the Son of man were risen from the dead" (Mark 9:9).

68 / Myth: The Jews Rejected Jesus As Messiah!

Why did he constantly command those who were excited about His supernatural abilities to "tell no man?" The Jews were not rejecting Jesus as Messiah, it was Jesus who was refusing to be the Messiah to the Jews!

Jews For Jesus

There were many Jews for Jesus when Christ fed 5000 with two biscuits and five sardines! Anyone who could feed that many people with so little, could feed an army that could fight Rome. Anyone who could heal leprosy could heal a soldier wounded in combat. Anyone who could raise Lazarus from the dead could raise a dead soldier who fought in his army. This Nazarene had something going for him that Rome couldn't match! Make no mistake about it, there were multiplied thousands of Jews for Jesus while he was walking on water, feeding the masses and raising the dead.

He performed these miracles to minister to the needs of the people, it was not intended to be a demonstration of supernatural signs to prove he was the Messiah. Every miracle Jesus did for the people they had seen before in the Hebrew Covenant. The signs Moses used to verify he was indeed God's leader for Israel had never been seen before.

The multiplied thousands who followed Jesus did not give up the idea he would be their Messiah until they saw Him hanging from a Roman Cross. Even after His resurrection and His repeated denials that He would not be the Messiah, His disciples were still hanging on to the last thread of hope that He would now smash

Myth: The Jews Rejected Jesus As Messiah!

Rome (Acts 1:6). The Jews for Jesus wanted Him to be their Messiah but He flatly refused!

The Jewish Mother

There is nothing like a pushy Jewish mother! The mother of James and John wanted Jesus to be Messiah. Right up until the shadow of His cross fell across the bloody sands of Calvary, the mother of James and John put on a full court press trying to get Jesus to agree to place her two sons at his right hand and at his left hand whenever He entered His kingdom. (Matthew 20:20-28).

She was not thinking about a Roman Cross, she was thinking about positions of influence and power for her sons in an earthly political kingdom. When Jesus defeated Rome as the Jewish Messiah, ushering in an era of universal peace, she wanted her sons in positions of power.

What was Jesus response?

He looked at this presumptuous Jewish mother and said, "You don't know what you're asking for your two sons. I didn't come to be ministered unto (to rule), I came to die!" (Matthew 20:28).

Two Disciples On Emmaus Road

The two disciples on the Road to Emmaus (located eight miles outside Jerusalem) wanted Jesus to be the Messiah. They were Cleopas, the father of James the less and his wife, Mary. As they walked, Jesus himself joined them but they did not recognize Him.

70 / Myth: The Jews Rejected Jesus As Messiah!

Jesus asked them, "What are you discussing together as you walk along?"

"Are you the only one living in Jerusalem who doesn't know the things that are happening here in these days? Cleopas asked.

"What things?" Jesus responded.

"About Jesus of Nazareth." they replied. "He was a prophet, powerful in word and deed before God and all the people. The chief priest and our ruler handed him over to be sentenced to death and they crucified him; *but we had hoped that He was the one that was going to redeem Israel.*" (Luke 24:17-21 NIV)

The two disciples on the Road to Emmaus had not rejected Jesus as Messiah ... their hopes were dashed!

It was not until Jesus entered their house for fellowship, as it was late in the evening, that they recognized Him. When he sat at their table, lifting His hands to bless and break the bread (Luke 24:35) they saw His nail-scarred hands and recognized Jesus. He instantly disappeared! He refused to be their Messiah, choosing to be the Savior of the world.

The Last Supper

Christians have little understanding of our Jewish roots and become confused when discussing the Last Supper and the Passover. Most think they are one and the same. They are not!

There are four days of preparation for Passover beginning at the tenth of Nisan or April. At sunset on

Myth: The Jews Rejected Jesus As Messiah! / 71

the tenth of the month, a series of three evening meals begin, all of which are served with leavened bread and fermented foods.

The first evening meal on the tenth of the month is called the "Feast of the First Night." The second meal served on the eleventh of the month is called the "Feast of the Second Night." The third meal which is served on the twelfth of the month is called the "Feast of the Third Night." The next night, on the thirteenth of the month at sunset, the last meal with leavened bread and fermented foods was eaten before Passover, which was the following evening, the fourteenth of Nisan or April. The last meal where leavened bread and fermented foods could be served was called the Last Supper. It is the night before Passover and is separate in purpose and meaning.

St. John describes Jesus dipping leavened bread into a "sop" which Judas took before leaving the Last Supper to betray the Lord. While the other gospels mention articles of Passover, John verifies that the betrayal took place at the time of the Last Supper. If it had been Passover, the High Priest who paid thirty pieces of silver to Judas would never have executed any kind of economic transaction on such a holy day.

After the eating of the Last Supper at which he was betrayed, Jesus celebrated the Passover the next evening at sundown with His disciples, minus Judas. It was here that He uniquely rejects for the final time the Messiahship of Israel.

It has been my priviledge to join the Orthodox Synagogue in San Antonio in the celebration of

72 / Myth: The Jews Rejected Jesus As Messiah!

Passover with Rabbi Arnold Schienberg. There are four cups of wine served at the Passover with a meal that symbolizes the tears and suffering of the Hebrew slaves in Egypt.
* The first cup is the cup of Rememberance!
* The second cup is the cup of Redemption!
* The third cup is the cup of Salvation!
* The fourth cup is the cup of Messiah!

When Jesus and His disciples came to the final cup during their last celebration of the Passover, *Jesus refused to drink* the Messiah's cup (Luke 22:17-18). He told His disciples, "Take this cup (Messiah's cup) and divide it among yourselves, for I say unto you, I will not drink of the fruit of the vine, until the Kingdom of God shall come."

In refusing to drink the cup, Jesus rejected to the last detail the role of Messiah in word or deed! The Jews did not reject Jesus as Messiah, it was Jesus who rejected the Jewish desire for Him to be their Messiah.

CHAPTER FIVE
MYTH: THE CHURCH HAS REPLACED ISRAEL

Replacement theologians are teaching over their pulpits that "God is finished with Israel. Israel is rejected and replaced by the Church to carry out the work once entrusted to Israel. Israel has ceased to be God's people and the Church is now spiritual Israel."

This theological anti-Semitism began with the transfer of the base of the early church from Jewish membership to a large gentile majority. The earliest Christians were Jewish who received the Great Commission to go into all the world and preach the gospel "to every creature." That meant the unclean Gentiles.

St. Paul clearly states that before the Jews brought the gospel to the Gentiles, the Gentiles walked in total spiritual darkness.

... without Christ, being aliens from the commonwealth of Israel, and strangers from the covenants of promise, having no hope, and without God in the world: But now in Christ Jesus you who once were afar off have been made near by the blood of Christ. For He Himself is our peace, who has made both one, and has broken down the middle wall of division between us (Ephesians 2:12-14).

Theological anti-Semitism began to teach in the first century that "the church is the new Israel" because the Gentile converts resented the priority of the Jewish people in the economy of God. The spirit of arrogance and pride cause this theology of hate to flourish today. It appeals to the ego to say, "We are the only people of God!"

Hitler sold this idea to the German people when he screamed to his enraptured audience, "We are the true people of God." The Japanese call themselves the "sons of heaven." Of course, every American knows they are both crazy because God sits on His throne waving the Stars and Stripes and "loves us best."

Listen to the message coming over the pulpits of America's 192 brands of Christianity. The message is very clear, "God loves my denomination best." This is a narcissistic theology that is a cancer of the soul.

The Biblical truth is that Our Father in Heaven loves us all. He is not the enemy of my enemies. God is not even the enemy of His enemies for the Bible teaches to "love your enemies." I know it's a shocking truth, but God even loves the people who are not in your denomination.

As soon as one adopts this ego gratifying theology that we are "the only people of God," he must turn on the Jews with a vengeance because the Bible plainly identifies them as "the Chosen People!" You can't both be "the only people of God."

Replacement theology is not a new revelation... it's an old heresy. In the *Epistles* of Ignatius of Antioch (ca. 70-107), he presents the church as "the new Israel." He also portrays the prophets and heros of Israel as "Christians before their time" and not part of the Jewish religion. The Church Fathers portrayed Balaam, Absolum and Judas as real Jews!

Myth: The Church Has Replaced Israel / 75

Replacement theologians *must use the allegorical method* of interpreting Scripture. This method was taught in Alexandria and based on the Platonic doctrine of ideas. This doctrine of ideas *spiritualizes the Biblical text* and avoids the historical and literal meaning of the text. Using the allegorical method of Biblical interpretation you can create a theology that says anything you want it to say. It's not truth ... it's God's Word twisted to tell a lie.

Using the allegorical method of scriptural interpretation you can prove King David rode a motorcycle through the main streets of Jerusalem. The Bible says, "King David's *triumph* was known throughout all Israel ... " The preacher who uses the allegorical method of Scriptural interpretation can say, "Friends, we all know that Triumph is the name brand of a motorcycle. Therefore, the Bible says King David rode a motorcycle through the streets of Jerusalem." The agony of this satire is that many of his congregants would believe him.

Those who teach that "the church is the new Israel" must use the allegorical method of Scriptural interpretation. It is the theology of space cadets! It is not possible to examine the *literal statements* of the Biblical text and conclude that God is finished with Israel and the church has taken her place.

Scripture plainly indicates that the Church (spiritual Israel) and national Israel exist side by side and neither replaces the other, EVER!

"Comfort Ye My People"

There are two Israel's in the scripture! One is a physical Israel, with a physical people, a physical Jerusalem and physical borders that are plainly defined in scripture. There is also a spiritual Israel, with a spiritual people, and a spiritual New Jerusalem. Spiritual Israel (the church) may have the blessings of physical Israel, but it does not replace physical Israel in the economy of God.

This is clearly seen in Isaiah 40:1 which states; "*Comfort ye*, comfort ye *my people*, saith your God."

The question must be asked, "Who is the "ye" of verse one?" It's plural so it's not one person, it's a body of people. There is a second group of people referred to as "my people." "My people" is also plural. There are in fact two groups of people in this verse. One group is being comforted and the other is the comforter.

Common logic will tell you that you cannot be the one who is *being comforted* and also be *the comforter*. The people being comforted in this verse is "my people," which is physical Israel! The one doing the comforting ("comfort ye") is spiritual Israel, the church.

These two Israels will merge together not one day sooner than when the Messiah literally comes to the physical city of Jerusalem. The prophet Zechariah describes the coming of Messiah and the Jewish reception of Messiah (Zechariah 12:10).

There are Replacement theologians in America preaching "that if Christians will quit supporting to Israel and will economically boycott the Christ

Myth: The Church Has Replaced Israel / 77

rejecting Jews, they will accept Jesus Christ."[1] An economic boycott of national Israel is not going to hasten the day the Jews convert and become spiritual Israel. This anti-Semitic logic defies and ignores both history and the Bible.

The Jews were economically attacked by Crusaders who robbed them of their last dime in the name of God ... they didn't become Christians. The Jews of the Spanish Inquisition were robbed of all their wealth as church and state split the plunder ... they did not become Christians. Adolf Hitler economically brought the Jews to their knees by forbidding them to have jobs, destroying their places of businesses in the infamous "Night of Glass" and then fined them billions of Marks to repair the damage his Nazi hoodlums inflicted upon the Jews ... they did not become Christians. He finally systematically slaughtered six million of them ... as they walked to the gas chamber they sang Hatkivah, not Amazing Grace! They did not become Christians.

It is time for Christians everywhere to know that the nation of Israel *will never convert to Christianity.*

- Yes, "all Israel will be saved" (Romans 11:26).
- Yes, Israel will welcome the Messiah (Zech 12:10)
- Yes, Israel will come to repentance (Romans 11:27).

But the idea that the Jews of the world are going to convert and storm the doors of Christian churches is a myth. After two thousand years of a loveless, Godless, anti-Semitic Christianity that has saturated the soil of the earth with their blood in the Crusades, the

78 / Myth: The Church Has Replaced Israel

Inquisition and the Holocaust, they are not about to convert. After two thousand years of an anti-Semitic Replacement theology that says "the church is the real Israel," thus denying the Jews their rightful place in the economy of God, they are not about to convert. Where is the Christianity that says "Love thy neighbor as thyself?" Where is the Christianity that says, "love does its neighbor no ill?" Where is the Christianity that "loves one another as I have loved you?" When the Jews see that kind of Christianity in action they will hear the footsteps of Messiah.

It is not the Jews and Judaism that have lost their credibility, it is a loveless Christianity that has lost its credibility! The Jews ask, "Was Jesus a false Messiah?" No one can be the true Messiah whose followers felt compelled to hate, murder, rob and rape for two thousand years and then brazenly proclaim "we are the people of God."

If Replaced, Why Reborn?

For eighteen hundred years, the Church Fathers ranted that "the church is the new Israel." To prove that God had turned His back upon the Jews, they pointed to the wandering, tormented Jews of the Diaspora saying, "If God is with them, why has this befallen them?"

Forget that the Jews were living for the most part in Papal States controlled by the Church of Rome. They lived without rights, without property, without legal

Myth: The Church Has Replaced Israel / 79

redress, and without human dignity in an environment created by the laws of the Church.

Replacement theologians ignore a fundamental fact in the Biblical text. When God replaces something, *you never hear from it again.* It is twice dead, plucked up by the roots and cast over the wall to be burned and forever forgotten.

On May 15, 1948, a theological earthquake leveled Replacement theology when national Israel was reborn after 2000 years of wandering. From the four corners of the earth the seed of Abraham began to return to the Land of their fathers. They returned "from their gentile graves" speaking sixty different languages and founded a nation that has become a super power in forty years. Israel is not passing away, it's building, growing, inventing, developing and the desert is blooming as the rose, just as the prophets of Israel promised.

The question must be asked, "If God was finished with the Jews and Israel, if they were in truth a cast off relic of the past without divine purpose or destiny, why did He allow that nation to be miraculously reborn? If replaced, why re-born?"

Their rebirth was living prophetic proof that Israel is not replaced. They were "reborn in a day" (Isa 66:8) to form the Third Commonwealth of Israel that shall endure until the coming of Messiah.

The Prophets Rebut Replacement Theology

If Israel as a nation had not been reborn, if the Jews had not returned to the land, if the cities of Israel had not been re-built, if Judea and Samaria (West Bank) had not been occupied, if the trees had not been replanted that the Turks cut down, if the agricultural accomplishments of Israel had not been miraculous, there would be a valid reason for every person to doubt that the Word of God is true. Listen to God's Word and His prophets declare His intention for the Jews of the world to inhabit Israel.

Isaiah Speaks!

"Do not be afraid, for I have redeemed you. I will bring your offspring from the east and gather you from the west. To the north I will say, "Give them up," and to the south, "Do not hold them." Bring my sons from far away, my daughters from the end of the earth" (Isaiah 43:5-6).

"They will come to Zion (Jerusalem) shouting for joy, everlasting joy on their faces; joy and gladness will go with them and sorrow and lament will be ended." (Isa. 35:10)

"They will rebuild the ancient ruins; they will raise what has long lain waste; they will restore the ruined cities, all that has lain waste for ages past. (Isa 61:4)

"I am he who says of Jerusalem, let her be inhabited, and let the towns of Judah, let them be rebuilt, and I shall raise them from their ruins once more. (Isa. 44:26)

Ezekiel Speaks!

"I am going to take you from among the gentiles and gather you together from all the foreign countries and

Myth: The Church Has Replaced Israel / 81

bring you to your own land. I will repopulate the cities and cause the ruins to be rebuilt. Desolate land will be tilled instead of laying waste under the eyes of every passer-by; till men say, this land once so desolate, is like a Garden of Eden today, and the ruined towns, once abandoned and leveled to the ground, are now strongholds with people living in them." (Ezek. 24-35)

"And they shall no longer be a prey for the nations, nor shall beasts of the land devour them; but they shall dwell safely, and no one shall make them afraid. I will raise up for them a garden of renown, and they shall no longer be consumed with hunger in the land, nor bear the shame of the Gentiles anymore. Thus they shall know that I, the Lord their God, am with them, and that they, the house of Israel, are My people." (Ezekiel 34:28-30)

"I will gather you together from the peoples. I will bring you back from the countries where you have been scattered, and I will give you the land of Israel . . . I will give them a single heart and I will put a new spirit in them." (Ezekiel 11:17-19)

"Therefore says the Lord God: 'Now I will bring back the captives of Jacob, and have mercy on the whole house of Israel; and I will be jealous for My holy name. After they have born their shame, and all their unfaithfulness in which they were unfaithful to Me, when they dwelt safely in their own land and no one made them afraid. When I have brought them back from the peoples and gathered them out of their enemies' lands, and I am hallowed in them in the sight of many nations, then they shall know that I am the Lord their

God, who sent them into captivity among the nations, but also brought them back to their own land, and left none of them captive any longer." (Ezekiel 37:21-28)

Jeremiah Speaks!

"Jacob's exiles I will restore. I will take pity on their homes. Towns will be rebuilt on their own sites and buildings stand where they once stood. (Jeremiah 30:18)
"Listen nations ... he who scattered Israel has gathered him ... for the Lord has ransomed Jacob, rescued him from a hand stronger than his own. They will come and shout for joy on the heights of Zion." (Jeremiah 31:10-12)
"I will restore the fortunes of my people Israel and Judah, the Lord says, and bring them back to possess the land I gave to their ancestors ... Do not be afraid, Israel, I will rescue you from far-off lands and your descendants from the countries where they are held captives ... The Lord has saved his people, the remnant of Israel. See, I bring them back from the land of the north and gather them from the far ends of the earth." (Jeremiah 30:3-31:8)

King David Speaks!

"When the Lord brings his people home, what joy for Jacob, what happiness for Israel." (Psa.14:7)
"When the Lord brought Zion's captives home, at first it seemed like a dream. Then our mouths filled

Myth: The Church Has Replaced Israel / 83

with laughter and our lips with song. Even the gentiles marveled at what the Lord had done for us." (Psa. 126:1-2)

(Psa. 107: 1-3) "Oh, give thanks to the Lord, for He is good! For His mercy endures forever. Let the redeemed of the Lord say so, Whom He has redeemed from the hand of the enemy, and *gathered out of the lands,* from the east and from the west, from the north and from the south."

Zechariah Speaks!

"Cry out this, says the Lord of Hosts, I am exceedingly jealous for Jerusalem and Zion, but bitterly angry against the proud nations, for while I was a little angry with Israel, they (the proud nations) overstepped all bounds. Therefore, the Lord says, I turn again in compassion to Jerusalem:: my Temple shall be rebuilt... my cities are once again going to be very prosperous, and the Lord will again comfort Zion and again make Jerusalem his very own." (Zech. 1:15-17)

"Jesus Rebuts Replacement Theology"

Jesus was the greatest teacher of the ages. He gave us three chapters (Matthew 24, Mark 13 and Luke 21) that are prophetic and present the events of the future in chronological order from the time He was speaking until His Second Coming. In Matthew chapter twenty-four, the disciples ask Jesus three questions;

1) "When shall these things be?" This question referred to the destruction of the Temple that he and the

84 / Myth: The Church Has Replaced Israel

Twelve had just left. Jesus answered in Luke 21:20 "But when you see Jerusalem surrounded by armies, then know that its desolation is near." This was accomplished in 70 A.D. when the Roman General Titus destroyed Jerusalem.
2) "What will be the sign of your coming?"
3) "And of the end of the age?" This world is coming to an end in spite of the Kingdom Now theology that says the church is going to become so victorous we will usher in the Millenial Age. Paul says in Galatians 1:4 "... that he (Jesus Christ) might *deliver us* from this present evil age, according to the will of our God and Father.

Let's move to Matthew 24:15 where Jesus is describing the Great Tribulation that will come upon the earth. This verse assumes that Israel is home and in control of the Holy Places.

"Therefore when you (the Jews) see the 'abomination of desolation,' spoken of by Daniel the prophet, standing in the holy place ...

The "holy place" is the Temple in Jerusalem. The Jews are in control of the Temple. How could they control the Temple without being in control of Jerusalem? How could they be in control of Jerusalem if they were replaced?

Jesus continues in verse sixteen by saying;

"then let those who are in Judea flee to the mountains."

Judea is what the media calls the West Bank. Jesus statement assumes that in the last days the Jews would be living on the West Bank. Jesus is describing in

Myth: The Church Has Replaced Israel / 85

verses 16-20 a general evacuation of the population in and around Jerusalem from a military attack.

Jesus is saying, When this military attack happens, don't go to Jerusalem which is five minutes away for safety. You have less than five minutes to save your life. Flee to the mountains as a matter of civil defense.

Jesus continues with ...

"Let him who is *on the housetop* not come down to take anything out of his house. And let him who is *in the field* not go back to get his clothes. (v. 17-18)

The roofs in Israel then and now are flat. People store things on the roof and sometimes sleep there. There is an outside stair way to the ground. Jesus is saying, when this military attack happens, don't carry anything down from the roof. Just run for safety!

The fields in Israel were within eyesight of the house. Jesus said, when this happens don't even go to the house to get your clothes.

Jesus continues with ...

"But woe to those who are pregnant and to those with nursing babies in those days! And pray that your flight may not be in winter or on the Sabbath. (v. 19-20)

Why woe to those who are pregnant and with nursing babies? Because their escape would be much more difficult. Why pray that your escape be not in winter or on the Sabbath? An escape from a military attack or an incoming Russian Katusha rocket launched from Syria would arrive in Jerusalem in less than five minutes.

86 / Myth: The Church Has Replaced Israel

Escape in winter would be far more difficult. Why pray that your flight not be on the Sabbath? This verse again assumes that the religious Jews are in control of the government in Israel where the laws of the Sabbath are being strictly enforced. On the Sabbath in Israel everything shuts down! There is no transportation. Even the elevators in the hotels and high rise apartments shut down.

A Russian rocket attack upon Jerusalem where there is no transportation and where the elevators were shut down would lead to a blood bath.

Jesus confirms that the Jews are back in Israel in verse twenty-two when he says;

"And unless those days were shortened, no flesh would be saved; but *for the elect's sake* those days will be shortened."

The elect are the Jewish people!

If the prophets and Jesus were certain that Israel would return to the land ... if they were certain that Israel had not been cast aside and replaced in the economy of God, how is it that America's Replacement Theologians can't see it?

Replacement Theology is Idolatry!

Replacement Theology is idolatry! I Samuel 15:23 states, "For rebellion is as the sin of witchcraft, and stubborness is as iniquity *and idolatry.*"

Who is a stubborn man? He is a man who refuses to change his opinion even when it is in direct conflict with God's Words! A stubborn man has made an *idol*

Myth: The Church Has Replaced Israel / 87

of his opinion and is in open rebellion against God. Wherever there is stubborness there is rebellion, and where there is rebellion there is witchcaft which leads to seduction and deception of believers.

Christians would never dream of allowing their pastor to preach with a statue of Budda draped around his neck. That's open idolatry! But they think nothing of permitting their pastor, whose personal opinons about Israel which are exactly opposite of the Word of God, lead them into deep deception.

Has the church replaced Israel? Not in the opinion of Jesus and the prophets of Israel!

CHAPTER SIX
MYTH: THE JEWS HAVE NO RIGHT TO THE LAND OF ISRAEL!

The greatest controversy of this century is raging out of control in the Middle East and threatens to engulf the globe with an inferno called World War III. The catalyst of the controversy is contained in this question, "To whom does the land of Israel belong?"

Some Christians are teaching, "the Jews have no right to the land of Israel!" The Arabs vehemently declare, "The land belongs to us. Because of the Holocaust and world sympathy that followed, it was given by those who did not own it (the British) to those who had no right to it (the Jews)."

The Jewish people, the seed of Abraham, Isaac and Jacob thunder back, "Our forefathers came to this land first, they conquered it and developed it. It's our historic homeland from the beginning of time to this day!"

Who is right?

Who Owned The Land First?

Whenever a controversy exists over who is the rightful owner of a given piece of property, an Abstract of Title must be prepared by the title company to prove beyond all reasonable doubt who is the rightful owner.

Myth: The Jews Have No Right To The Land Of Israel!

An Abstract of Title must trace ownership of the property back to the first owner and then forward to the present owner, making certain that a clear and unclouded title is passed from one owner to the next from generation to generation. If the title has been passed properly from one owner to the next over the generations, then the present owner has a clear and unclouded title to that property. Thus the source of the question, "Who owned the land first?"

King David assists us in the preparation of this Abstract of Title by clearly identifying the original owner of the land as God.

"The earth is the Lord's and the fulness thereof; the world, and they that dwell therein" (Psalm 24:1).

"The land, moreover, shall not be sold permanently, for the land is mine ... " Leviticus 25:23

"In the beginning God created the heavens and the earth ... Genesis 1:1"

The Abstract of Title must go back to the very beginning. The first verse of the first chapter identifies God as the original land owner of all lands, including Israel. It was His to give to whomever He sovereignly chose.

God Records The Title Deed!

God said to Abraham at Hebron:
"Lift your eyes now and look from the place where you are ... northward, southward, eastward and westward; for all the land which you see I *give to*

you and to your descendants forever. Arise, walk the land through its length and its width, for I give it to you." (Genesis 13:14 & 17)

"On the same day the Lord made a covenant with Abram, saying: 'To your descendants I have given this land, from the river of Egypt to the great river, the River Euphrates." (Genesis 15:18)

"Also I give to you and your descendants after you the land in which you are a stranger, all the land of Canaan, as an *everlasting possession*; and I will be their God." (Genesis 17:8)

"And I will set your bounds (borders) from the Red Sea to the Sea of the Philistines (Mediterranean Sea), and from the desert to the Euphrates River." (Exodus 23:31)

Title Deed to Israel is Passed to Abraham

The world's most controversial real estate contract is recorded in exact detail in the pages of Genesis. God, the original owner, spoke to Abraham and said,

"Get thee out of thy father's house, unto a land that I will show you." (Genesis 12:1)

Abraham was separated from Ur, a city of idol worship, in obedience to God's command to leave. He was separated from his father by death, and was separated from Lot by contention. Abraham was now divinely positioned to receive title deed to the land of Israel.

"And the Lord said unto Abram ... lift up now thine eyes, and look from the place where thou art northward, and southward, and eastward, and

92 / Myth: The Jews Have No Right To The Land Of Israel!

westward: For all the land which thou seest, to *thee will I give it, and to thy seed forever"* (Genesis 13:14-15).

The unclouded title was passed to Abraham and his children forever from God. "Forever" means forever! The Jewish people have the Biblical mandate to possess the land of Israel today, tomorrow and as long as the sun rises and sets on planet Earth.

The Title Deed is valid regardless of the United Nations resolutions, the threats of the Soviet Union and its surrogate states in the Middle East, or the heinous terrorist attacks upon Israel. The Title Deed is recorded by God in the chronicles of heaven forever!

Title Passed to Isaac!

Abraham is also the father of Arab nations! His children through Sarah and Isaac are the Jews. His children through Hagar and Ishmael are the Arabs. What began as a family feud, between two brothers in the Middle East 6000 years ago, now threatens to engulf the world in war.

It was Abraham's desire to transfer the Royal Land Grant to Ishmael. God rejected Abraham's request!

"And Abraham said unto God, O that Ishmael might live before thee. And God said, Sarah thy wife shall bear thee a son indeed: and thou shalt call his name Isaac: and I will establish my covenant with him, and with his seed after him. And as for Ishmael, I have heard thee: Behold I have blessed him and will make him fruitful, and will

Myth: The Jews Have No Right To The Land Of Israel!

multiply him exceedingly; twelve princes shall he beget, and I will make him a great nation. But *my covenant will I establish with Isaac,* which Sarah shall bear thee at this set time in the next year" (Gen. 17:18-21).

God promised Abraham that he would bless Ishmael and make him a great nation. That blessing is obvious as the Arab nations have been the heirs of the richest oil fields in the world. It must be remembered that one need not be anti-Arab to be pro-Israel. God loves them both!

But concerning their inheritance, there can be no mistake in this Title Deed transfer. It went from Abraham to Isaac and his seed after him. The Apostle Paul confirms that Isaac was the recipient of the Title Deed to Israel: "In Isaac your descendants shall be called" (Hebrews 11:18).

Abraham had six other sons by his concubine, Keturah. Their heirs have stormed onto the stage of history in the Twentieth Century, demanding ownership of the land. Abraham's last will and testament eliminates the controversy created by the heirs of Keturah's sons with:

"And Abraham gave all that he had unto Isaac. But unto the sons of the concubines, which Abraham had, Abraham gave gifts, and *sent them away* from Isaac his son, while he yet lived, eastward unto the east country." (Genesis 25:5-6)

God confirmed again in Genesis 26:3-5 that the Title Deed to Israel had been passed from His seat of authority in Heaven to Abraham, to Isaac and was now ready to be passed to Jacob.

94 / Myth: The Jews Have No Right To The Land Of Israel!

Title Passed to Jacob!

Isaac and his beautiful wife, Rebecca, were expecting their firstborn. Isaac was sixty years of age when the Lord spoke to Rebecca and told her,
"Two nations are in thy womb, and two manner of people shall be parted from thy bowels: and the one people shall be stronger than the other people; and the elder shall serve the younger" (Genesis 25:23).

The phrase "the elder shall serve the younger" is critical to clear passage of the title. It was the Hebrew custom that the first born would receive the birthright from the father and be the legal head of the house for generations to come.

Esau was the firstborn, but God rejected him as heir to the Royal Land Grant. It was given to his younger twin brother, Jacob. God's rejection of Esau as heir to the land of Israel resounds in Romans 9:10-13 like a clap of thunder:
"And not only this; but when Rebecca had conceived by one, even our father Isaac; (for the children being not yet born, neither having done any good or evil, that the purpose of God according to election might stand, not of works but of him that calleth.) It was said unto her, The elder (Esau) shall serve the younger (Jacob). As it is written, Jacob have I loved, but Esau have I hated."

The Almighty and Omniscient God knew the character of Esau before he ever left his mother's womb. God knew that he would sell his priceless birthright for a mess of pottage. Jacob received the

Myth: The Jews Have No Right To The Land Of Israel! / 95

birthright from Isaac and later the Title Deed to the Royal Land Grant of Israel. It is recorded:

"And Isaac called Jacob and blessed him ... And God Almighty bless thee, and make thee fruitful, and multiply thee, that thou mayest be a multitude of people: and give thee the blessing of Abraham, to thee and to thy seed with thee; *that thou mayest inherit the land* wherein thou art a stranger, which God gave unto Abraham" (Gen. 28:1,3-4).

After Isaac blessed Jacob, God personally approved Jacob as the new holder to the Title Deed of the land of Israel. When Jacob left his family and Beersheba to escape the wrath of Esau, he spent the night at a place he called Bethel. This was to be one of the most important nights in the life of Jacob. As he slept, the Scripture records,

"And he dreamed, and behold, a ladder was set up on the earth, and its top reached to heaven; and there the angels of God were ascending and descending on it. And behold, the Lord stood above it, and said, "I am the Lord God of Abraham your father, and the God of Isaac; the land on which you lie *I will give to you and your descendants*" (Genesis 28:12-13).

Jacob made an altar of stones to mark the place where God had given him the Title Deed to Israel. He awoke the next morning, journeyed to the house of his greedy and deceitful uncle, Laban, where he entered into a working agreement which consumed fourteen years of his life. From this labor contract, Jacob

96 / Myth: The Jews Have No Right To The Land Of Israel!

gained two wives, one by deception on the part of Laban and one by desire.

Laban changed Jacob's wages ten times and each time to Jacob's hurt. God gave Jacob a unique breeding technique that produced spotted cattle and made him a mighty man of wealth. Tired of his father-in-law's treachery, he decided to return to the land that God had given him fourteen years earlier . . . the land of Israel. There, God confirmed a second time, at Bethel, His intention for Jacob to be the heir to the Royal Land Grant as recorded in Genesis 35:9-12.

The chronological listing of the persons involved in the passing of this Title Deed is repeated by Jacob's favorite son, Joseph, on his death bed in Egypt;

"And Joseph said to his brethren, "I am dying; but God will surely visit you, and bring you out of this land (Egypt) to the land (Israel) of which he swore to Abraham, to Isaac, and to Jacob." (Genesis 50:24)

Moses, the great Law Giver of Israel, maintained the integrity of the unclouded Title Deed when he wrote,

"Remember Abraham, Isaac and Israel (Jacob), Your servants, to whom You swore by Your own self, and said to them, 'I will multiply your descendants as the stars of the heaven; and all this land that I have spoken of I give to your descendants, and *they shall inherit it forever'"* Exodus 32:13).

How Much Land Is Covered In The Title Deed?

Cartographers, aided by ambitious warlords, have mapped and re-mapped the ever changing Middle East.

Myth: The Jews Have No Right To The Land Of Israel!

Before one set of boundaries can be internationally established with printed maps, the volatile Middle East again becomes involved in military conflict and with it, another set of maps and boundaries is required.

Presently, a controversy rages over Judea and Samaria, the West Bank, as it is referred to in the United Nations and the media. Who has legal claim to the West Bank? Do the Palestinians have the historic and legal right to claim it as their homeland. Or is it covered in the Title Deed that God passed to Abraham, Isaac and Jacob and their seed forever? The next critical question is: "How much land did God transfer to Abraham, Isaac and Jacob, and where are the boundaries set in the scripture?

The God of Heaven is a God of exactness and precision. His pinpoint description of the property that the Jews were to have "forever" is recorded in history's most important meets and bounds description in Genesis 15:18:

> "In the same day the Lord made a covenant with Abram, saying, Unto thy seed I have given this land, from the river of Egypt unto the great river, the river Euphrates."

Two boundaries are given here; the river of Egypt (Red Sea) and the Euphrates River. These boundaries exist today and clearly mark the west and east boundaries of the Royal Land Grant that God gave to the Jewish people.

The Red Sea is logically the place where God's promise came into effect.

Myth: The Jews Have No Right To The Land Of Israel!

"Every place whereon the soles of your feet shall tread shall be yours: from the wilderness and Lebanon, and from the river, the river Euphartes, even unto the uttermost Sea shall your coast be" (Deut. 11:24).

Two boundaries for this real estate gift from God to the Jewish people are now established. The boundary on the west side was the Red Sea which flows into the Mediterranean Sea, forming the complete western boundary.

The eastern boundary is the Euphrates River. Joshua confirms these western and eastern boundaries of Israel with;

"From the wilderness and this Lebanon even unto the great river, the river Euphrates, all the land of the Hittites, and unto the great sea (Mediterranean Sea) toward the going down of the sun (west) shall be your coast." (Joshua 1:4)

The northern border of Israel is established in Ezekiel 48:1 as the city of Hamath which can still be located on a quality map. The Biblical record reads:

"From the north end to the coast of the way of Hethlon, as one goeth to Hamath ... "

The southern boundary of Israel is established in Ezekiel 48:28. The Biblical record reads;

"And by the border of Gad, at the southside southward, the border shall be even from Tamar unto the waters of strife in Kadesh, and to the river (Red Sea) and toward the great sea (Mediterranean Sea).

Myth: The Jews Have No Right To The Land Of Israel!

The Royal Land Grant that God, the original owner, gave to Abraham, Isaac and Jacob and their seed forever, includes the following territory which is presently occupied by Israel, the West Bank, all of Lebanon, one half of Syria, two thirds of Jordan, all of Iraq, and the northern portion of Saudi Arabia.

It immediately becomes obvious why the enemies of Israel belittle the Word of God as a source of truth in settling this political controversy. When truth is rejected a man is committed to believing a lie.

What About The Homeless Palestinians?

This emotionally charged question is generally asked by someone who is aware that approximately 600,000 Palestinian Arabs were left homeless when Israel became a nation in 1948. The question is usually couched as a propaganda tool to portray the Jews in Israel as heartless people who expelled the Palestinians from their homes and refuse to allow them to resettle. All you have to do to believe this is to totally ignore the historical development of the Palestinian Refugees.

The British, who after the First World War succeeded the Turks as masters of Palestine (the Roman name for the Land of Israel), recognized the right of the Jewish people to reconstitute its country as a National Home and pledged to facilitate this in the Balfour Declaration. Under the Mandate, conferred upon Britain by the League of Nations, over half a million Jews

100 / *Myth: The Jews Have No Right To The Land Of Israel!*

returned to their ancestral land, either to fulfil an ancient ideal or to escape from the Nazi persecution.

The Mandatory period was, however, one of bitter strife. The British showed growing signs during the 1930s of going back on their earlier pledges to the Jewish people, and the White Paper issued on the eve of the Second World War effectively spelled an end to the Jewish National Home as provided in the Balfour Declaration.

The Jewish community in Palestine was prepared to shelve its dispute with Britain for the duration of the Second World War, and rallied strongly behind the Allied war effort with thousands of Palestinian Jews joining the Allied ranks.

In 1947, Britain decided to withdraw from Palestine, charging the United Nations with the task of finding a solution acceptable to both the Jews and Arabs.

On November 29, 1947, the General Assembly of the United nations decided to partition Palestine and create two independent states, one Arab and one Jewish. The leadership of the Jewish community in Palestine welcomed the decision, thereby expressing its willingness to live side by side with an independent Palestinian Arab state.

The Palestinian Arabs, however, flatly rejected the UN decision. Two days later, on December 1, 1947, they took up arms against the Jewish community. Their strategy was to attack outlying Jewish villages, Jewish institutions and vehicles driven by the Jews. These attacks, in which hundreds of Jews died, have been graphically described by Col. Abdallah Tal in his book

Myth: The Jews Have No Right To The Land Of Israel!

The Calamity of Palestine. Colonel Tal, of the Transjordanian Arab Legion, was himself responsible for training and arming the Palestinian Arabs.

For four months the Jews did not retaliate, hoping that the Palestinian Arabs would finally accept the UN partition plan. By April 1948, however, it was clear that this was not to be, and the Jews launched a counter-offensive. As the fighting spread, Arabs began abandoning their villages and towns to escape the hostilities. This marked the beginning of the Palestinian refugee problem.

On May 15, 1948, the day after the State of Israel was proclaimed, five Arab armies (Egypt, Transjordan, Syria, Lebanon and Iraq) invaded Palestine. This greatly escalated the refugee problem as Arab commanders told the Palestinians to leave their homes "for the duration of the war" until they had slaughtered the Zionists. More than 600,000 took this advice, fleeing to the neighboring Arab countries waiting for victory over Israel. They are still waiting!

When hostilities ended in 1949, the Egyptian and Transjordanian forces were in control of the bulk of the territory designated for the Arab state under the 1947 partition plan. Transjordan subsequently annexed Judea-Samaria, which became the "West Bank" of the Hashemite Kingdom of Jordan.

By the time hostilities ended in 1949, an estimated 660,000 Palestinian Arabs had become refugees. Israel permitted the return of refugees who wished to return with their families. In April 1949, at the UN Palestine Conciliation Commission at Lausanne,

102 / Myth: The Jews Have No Right To The Land Of Israel!

Israel offered to repatriate 100,000 Arab refugees within the framework of a general settlement. The Arab delegations rejected the offer.

In 1950, the United Nations Relief and Works Agency (UNRWA) proposed resettling Arab refugees in Sinai, Jordan and Syria, but the Arab Governments also rejected this proposal. In 1952, the UN Refugee Rehabilitation Fund offered the Arab States $200 million to find homes and jobs for the refugees. The Arab States did not even apply for the greater part of the fund.

In simple historic terms, the Palestinian Refugee Problem was created by the Arabs attacking the Jews, greatly accelerated when five Arab armies attacked Israel, May 15, 1948, telling the Palestinians to leave "for the duration of the war" and sustained because the Arab leaders do not want to resolve the pathetic plight of their own people. It makes a magnificent propaganda tool on international television to show the thousands of homeless Palestinian children living in squalor and blame it on the Jewish people.

The truth is, if the Arab states were willing, they could resettle the Arab refugees just as Israel has resettled its Jewish refugees from Nazi persecution.

Money is not lacking. The oil revenues of the Arab states, all of which are underpopulated, make the Arabs the most wealthy people per capita on the face of the earth.

Social integration poses no problem for the Palestinian Arabs speak the same language, and are of the same religion, ethnic stock and background as Arabs elsewhere in the Middle East.

Myth: The Jews Have No Right To The Land Of Israel! /103

When Americans sit before the television and see the pathetic plight of these poor people, they need to remember the historical truth of this tragedy ... the Arabs did this to their own people, not the Jews.

For those who are pounding their chest and demanding that Israel give back the land to which they have a Biblical Mandate ... forget it! The Title Deed to Israel has been recorded by the hand of Jehovah God and the seed of Abraham shall possess it *forever!*

CHAPTER SEVEN
MYTH: "THE OLD COVENANT IS DEAD"!

Replacement theology advances the concept that the Old Testament has been replaced by the New Testament. The Old Testament is presented in a manner that suggests it is an inferior approach to God, as being harsh, cold, legalistic, justice without mercy and fostering fear without compassion. The intimation is that it should be disregarded by New Testament Christians who have the superior light and love.

Need we be reminded that the loving theology of the New Testament, as translated by the Church Fathers, sponsored the Crusades, the Inquisition and ultimately produced the Holocaust?

Replacement theologians are now saying, "The Old Covenant must likewise be put to death. God cannot, will not, has never before and never will be in covenant with more than one people."[1] Translation: The Old Testament is dead and the Jews have no place in the economy of God!

Is that what the Bible teaches?

What is a Covenant?

In the Bible, the meaning of covenant is wrapped up in the Hebrew word Berit. It means a contract, a will, a testament, or a bond. A covenant in the Scripture cannot be revoked, altered, annulled or replaced by a new covenant. A new covenant can enhance, extend, or com-

106 / Myth: "The Old Covenant Is Dead!"

pliment the former covenant, but it never replaces the former covenant.

A covenant is not to be confused with a vow. A vow can be broken by certain conditions of revocation. A covenant, once spoken into existence, is everlasting.

Three Types of Covenant

There are three kinds of covenant recorded in the Scripture. They are the:
1) Shoe Covenant (Ruth 4:7)
2) Salt Covenant (Lev. 2:13 Numbers 18:19)
3) Blood Covenant (Gen. 15:7-18 Matt. 26:28)

The most common type of covenant was the shoe covenant. Whenever someone in Israel wanted to enter a contract to perform a specific task, he would give his shoe or sandal to the person entering into the covenant with him.

If you've been to Israel, you know that it's impossible to go very far without your shoes. The terrain is covered with sharp, jagged rocks and blazing hot sand. The first time I was in Israel, I knew immediately why stoning was the method of capitol punishment. Rocks are everywhere! All you have to do to find plenty is bend over and reach down.

When you gave your shoe to someone on this rocky terrain in an act of covenant, you were saying, "I won't be far from this spot when you come looking for me."

When Boaz came before the elders to redeem Ruth from her near kinsman, he took off his sandal and gave

Myth: "The Old Covenant Is Dead!" / 107

it to the near kinsman, and expressed his desire to marry Ruth. This was the shoe covenant in Israel.

The salt covenant was a covenant of loyalty. Salt was carried by everyone in Israel in a small pouch tied to the belt. When the sun's heat caused a loss of body salt through perspiration, the individual would take a pinch of salt to prevent muscle cramps.

The salt covenant was made by the contracting parties as they reached into their respective pouches to get a pinch of salt to exchange with the person entering into the covenant. As they exchanged salt by placing it in the other person's pouch, they would recite the contents of the covenant they were making. It was unthinkable in Scripture for those who entered the salt covenant to be disloyal to each other even if they had been bitter enemies. Their covenant of loyalty was expressed by saying, "There is salt between us!"

After exchanging salt, they would shake their individual pouches to thoroughly mix the grains of salt. The significance of this salt covenant was that as long as the grains of salt were mixed, the contract stands. Technically, the only way the contract could be terminated was for each of the contracting parties to retrieve their exact grains of salt from the other person involved. This was impossible once the salt pouches were ceremoniously shaken.

The third kind of covenant in Scripture was the blood covenant. It was used only in the most urgent contracts. It consisted of dividing the carcass of an animal or animals in half and placing the halfs on the right hand and left hand making an aisle between them. The persons entering into this most urgent covenant walked back and forth between the pieces of the sacrifice and recited the contents of the covenant. The symbolism, as expressed by the animal whose blood had been spilled and whose body had been split in half, was that if either party broke the covenant their blood should be spilled and their body split in half.

There are two significant blood covenants recorded in the Bible. The first was between God and Abraham, giving Abraham and his seed through Isaac and Jacob the land of Israel forever. The second was the shed blood of the Lamb of God at Calvary removing the curse of sin from all humanity.

God's Blood Covenant With Abraham For The Royal Land Grant of Israel!

When God passed the Title Deed of Israel to Abraham and his seed through Isaac and Jacob forever, He did so with the most spectacular blood covenant recorded in the Old Testament.

"And he (God) said unto him, (Abraham) I am the Lord that brought thee out of Ur of the Chaldees, to give thee this land to inherit it. And he said, Lord God, whereby shall I know that I shall inherit it. And he said unto him, Take me an heifer of three years old, and a she goat of three years old, and a ram of three years old, and a turtle dove and a young pigeon. And he took unto him all these, and divided them in the midst (split them in half), and laid each piece one against the other: but the birds divided he not. And when the fowls came

Myth: "The Old Covenant Is Dead!" / 109

down upon the carcases, Abram drove them away. And when the sun was going down, a deep sleep fell upon Abram: and lo, an horror of great darkness fell upon him." (Genesis 15:7-18)

The contracting parties in this blood covenant were Jehovah God and Abraham. Abraham slew the heifer, the goat, the ram and the birds and laid their carcasses out on the ground, preparing to enter into the blood covenant concerning the land of Israel. God instructed Abraham to slaughter and divide many animals because this was to be the most important real estate covenant in the history of mankind. It would be a covenant that nations would contest and theologians would condemn.

At sundown, God placed Abraham into a "deep sleep." It was an anesthesia exactly like He used upon Adam, when He removed his rib to form Eve, in the first recorded organ transplant. God put Abraham in a "deep sleep" for no man can look upon God and live.

"And it came to pass, when the sun went down and it was dark, that behold, there was a smoking furnace and a burning lamp that passed between those pieces. On the same day the Lord made a covenant with Abram, saying: 'To your descendants I have given this land, from the river of Egypt (Red Sea) to the great river, the River Euphrates ... " (Genesis 15:17-18)

In his sleep, Abraham saw "a smoking furnace and the burning lamp that passed between those pieces." In the Old Testament, the burning lamp signified the presence of the Shekinah glory of God. God Himself,

110 / *Myth: "The Old Covenant Is Dead!"*

apart from Abraham's participation or promise, was binding Himself in a blood covenant to fulfill that which He had promised to Abraham. The dimensions of the land are clearly stated as being from the Nile River to the Euphrates River and from the Persian peninsula to Asia Minor.

If God has broken His blood covenant with Abraham, as Replacement theologians are teaching, what confidence can we have that He will keep the blood covenant of the Cross? Both covenants were made by the same God! If God is a covenant breaker, he lied to Abraham and to David. If God is a covenant breaker and has cast aside the Old Testament for the New Testament, how can we be sure He won't cast aside the New Testament? If God is a covenant breaker, every Bible believer on planet Earth must go to bed tonight knowing that our sins are not forgiven, the blood sacrifice of the Lamb of God at Calvary was in vain, and that the Biblical text is utter rubbish composed by a God who cannot keep His word! That is the message of Replacement theology!

God's Covenant With Abraham Creating The Nation Of Israel

The Abrahamic Covenant (Gen. 12:1-3) was restricted to the seed of Abraham through Isaac and Jacob. This covenant established Israel as a nation and is *everlasting and unconditional.* Unconditional means this covenant is contingent upon God's faithfulness to Israel, not Israel's faithfulness to God. God says five

Myth: "The Old Covenant Is Dead!" / 111

times in this covenant, "I will, I will, I will." He never says to Abraham, "You must ... you must!" The covenant reads,

"Now the Lord had said to Abram: 'Get thee out of your country, From your kindred And from your father's house, To a land that *I will* show you. *I will* make you a great nation; *I will* bless you and make your name great; And you shall be a blessing. *I will* bless those who bless you, and *I will* curse him who curses you; and in you all the families of the earth will be blessed."

There are seven specific sections of this covenant. They are;
1) A land that I will show you
2) I will make of thee a great nation
3) I will bless thee
4) I will make thy name great
5) Thou shalt be a blessing
6) I will bless them that bless thee and curse them that curse thee
7) In thee shall all the families of the earth be blessed.

An Unconditional Covenant

The Christians who are now saying that God broke His covenant with Israel are ignoring the Scripture written by King David. He says the covenant was unconditional.

"If his children (the Jews) forsake my law, and walk not in my judgements; If they break my

Myth: "The Old Covenant Is Dead!"

statutes, and keep not my commandments; then will I visit their transgressions with the rod, and their iniquity with stripes. Nevertheless, my loving kindness will I not utterly take from him, nor suffer my faithfulness to fail. My covenant will I not break, nor alter the thing that has gone out of my lips. Once I have sworn by my holiness that I will not lie unto David. His seed shall endure forever, and his throne as the sun before me. It shall be established forever as the moon, and as a faithful witness in heaven. Selah." (Psalm 89:30-37)

Jehovah God promised Israel that if you break my statutes, my commandments and my law, I will punish you with a rod and stripes. The pages of history are laden with the anguish of the Jews. They have passed under the rod of God's judgement . . . but His unconditional covenant holds!

God uses the sun and the moon as witnesses that the covenant with the Jewish people stands. The witness of the sun and moon is a twenty-four hour reminder for anyone, anywhere on planet Earth, who can look up and see the blinding light of the sun or the reflected light of the moon. As long as man can see either of them, Israel has a covenant with God.

Moses confirms that God keeps covenant forever. He wrote;

"Therefore know that the Lord your God, He is God, the faithful God who keeps covenant and mercy for a thousand generations with those who love Him and keep His commandments." (Deuteronomy 7:9)

Myth: "The Old Covenant Is Dead!" / 113

God keeps covenant for a thousand generations! A thousand generations technically is 40,000 years but is an expression of speech which means forever. God is a God of covenant.

Hebrews 10:9

Those Replacement theologians, anxious to prove that the Old Testament is dead and replaced by the New Testament, race to Hebrews 10:9 to justify their position.

"Previously saying, 'Sacrifice and offering, burnt offerings, and offerings for sin You did not desire, nor had pleasure in them' (Which are offered according to the law), then He said, 'Behold, I have come to do your will, O God.' *He takes away the first that He may establish the second.*"

Hebrew scholar, Vendyl Jones, responds, "Commentators from the medieval monks to the modern translators and theologians teach that this passage means that God's will in Jesus was to take away the "old" Jewish system and establish the new Christian system. The Greek word translated "taketh away" is anairo, which means "to slay," or "to kill." That would make the argument even stronger for the Replacement theologian except for one consideration: the context is not dealing with the old 'covenant' and the new 'covenant.' The context is discussing Yom Kippurim, or the Day of Atonement. Only on one day a year was the Golden Censer placed behind the Second Veil, or in the Holy of Holies, and that day was Yom Kippurim.

114 / Myth: "The Old Covenant Is Dead!"

Exodus 25 and 37 indicate that the Golden Censer was ordinarily placed in the Holy Place, not the Holy of Holies. It sat between the Menorah and the Table of Shewbread *in front of* the Second Veil. Hebrews 9:4 describes it as being behind the Second Veil in the Holy of Holies, indicating the special occasion (Yom Kippurim or Day of Atonement).

Because of lack of knowledge of Judaism, however, the commentators argue that this reference contains a mistake, or that a Gentile who did not know the Jewish law wrote Hebrews. Therefore, they insinuate that Paul or Barnabus certainly could not have written the epistle. Since the context of Hebrews 9-10 is the first Tabernacle and second, the Temple, they continue and insert the word covenant so that the latter covenant in Christ replaced the former covenant of Israel. There is no such indication in the text.

Hebrews 9:4 does not contain a mistake! It refers particularly to the censer's special location in the Holy of Holies on Yom Kippurim, the one day of the year on which the censer is moved from the front of the veil (Lev. 16:12). On that one day, the high priest offered a bull for himself and two goats for the people (Hebrews 9:13, Lev. 16:1-34). On the Day of Atonement the two goats, *not the two covenants*, were taken. The first lots fell on the goat of the Eternal One; the latter lots fell on Azazel Yisrael, the scapegoat for Israel. The high priest 'killeth the first goat,' not the first covenant, and the second goat, not the new covenant, was taken away and established, or kept alive, as the scapegoat of Israel."[2]

Myth: "The Old Covenant Is Dead!" / 115

The Old Testament Replaced?

I repeat, when something is replaced in the plan of God it is plucked up by the roots, cast over the wall, burned and buried, never to be heard of again. If the Old Testament is replaced by the New Testament, why do the Ten Commandments appear in the New Testament? By an honest investigation of Scripture anyone can soon determine that there are nine of the ten commandments in the New Testament. The 4th commandment, which refers to the Sabbath, is not found because the New Covenant permits any day to be observed as a day of rest and worship (Romans 14:5-6, Gal. 4:9-10 and Col. 2:14-17).

New Testament scriptures incorporating the Ten Commandments of God as given through Moses are:

I) Exodus 20:3 wi:2-3; col. 3:20, 2 Tim. 3:2
II) Exodus 20:4-6 with Romans 2:22 I Cor. 5:10; 6:9-11
III) Exodus 20:7 with Acts 26:11: Romans 2:24; Col. 3:8
IV) Exodus 20:8-10 (Law of Sabbath not commanded in the New Covenant)
V) Exodus 20:12 with Ephesians 6:2-3; Col. 3:20, 2 Tim. 3:2
VI) Exodus 20:13 with Romans 13:9; I Peter 4:15; I John 3:15
VII) Exodus 20:14 with Romans 2:22; 13:9; I Cor. 6:9-11
VIII) Exodus 20:15 with Romans 2:21; 13:9; Eph. 4:28

116 / *Myth: "The Old Covenant Is Dead!"*

IX) Exodus 20:16 with Romans 13:9
X) Exodus 20:17 with Romans 13:9; I Cor. 5:10; 6:9-11 etc.

Again, if the Old Testament is dead, why does it live in the New Testament? If the Old Testament is dead, why did Jesus use it as a foundation for His teaching in His earthly ministry? Jesus said, "Thou shalt love thy neighbor as thyself" (Matthew 19:19). Where did He get that doctrine? Was it revelation knowledge? No! It's a verbatim quote from Moses who said, "Thou shalt love thy neighbor as thyself" (Leviticus 19:18).

The Apostle Paul continues to teach the law of love in Romans 13:9 with ... "thou shalt love thy neighbor as thyself." James records the theme by saying, "If you really fulfill the royal law according to the Scripture, 'You shall love your neighbor as yourself,'" you do well.

What is the source of all this New Testament superior light? It comes from Moses and the Old Covenant that is supposed to be dead, useless and replaced!

Jesus Christ personally validated the divine authority of the Old Covenant by saying, "think not that I am come to destroy the Law, or the prophets: *I am not come to destroy*, but to fulfill" (Matthew 5:17). He continues in the next verse to declare that the Old Covenant would be valid "until heaven and earth passed away." Heaven and earth have not passed away, neither has the Old Covenant!

The Apostle Paul wrote: "*All scripture* is given by inspiration of God, and is *profitable* for doctrine, for reproof, for correction, for instruction in righteousness: that the man of God may be perfect, throughly furnished unto all

Myth: "The Old Covenant Is Dead!" / 117

good works" (2 Timothy 3:16-17). All scripture includes the Old Covenant!

Paul describes twenty three sins that are the result of apostasy in Romans 1:29-31. He states that men would be "covenantbreakers, without natural affection..." (meaning homosexuals and sodomites). If God is a covenantbreaker, He is listed as being apostate and catagorized with homosexuals and sodomites in His Word.

John gives a stern and shocking warning in the final chapter of the Revelation by saying, "For I testify to everyone who hears the words of the prophecy of this book (the Bible): If anyone adds to these things, God will add to him the plagues that are written in this book; and if *anyone takes away* from the words of the book of this prophecy, God shall take away his part from the Book of Life, from the holy city, and from the things which are written in this book" (22:18-19).

Replacement theology "takes away" thirty nine books from the Bible by calling the Old Testament dead and replaced. Those who do so are guaranteed to have their names removed from the Book of Life. The Old Covenant is the Word of God without which the New Covenant would be an absolute mystery.

CHAPTER EIGHT
THE MYSTERY OF ISRAEL!

The Apostle Paul refers to God's position on the Jews and Israel, as expressed in Romans chapters nine through eleven, as being a "mystery." Christians who tailor their religion to fit the pattern of their prejudice simply ignore these three chapters. Ignoring Scripture is not the same as interpreting Scripture.

Is it a "mystery" that we can't understand? No, Paul states that it is a mystery he wants the Gentiles to understand lest they become arrogant in their opinions and God's judgement falls on them.

"For I do not desire, brethren, that you should be
ignorant of this mystery, lest you should be wise
in your own opinion ... " (Romans 11:25)

What is a "mystery" in the Pauline epistles? Paul uses the word "mystery" again in I Corinthians 15:51-52 where he is explaining the mystery of the rapture of the church.

"Behold I tell you a mystery: We shall not all sleep,
but we shall be changed, in a moment, in the
twinkling of an eye, at the last trumpet."

A "mystery" in the Pauline epistles is a fact known by God from the beginning of time that is now being made known to man for the first time in the Word of God. It has been hidden until this moment and therefore has been a mystery. Now, in God's timing, He chooses to reveal to man the hidden truth.

The mystery of Israel is revealed in Romans 9-11 and while we may not understand God's purpose, we can know His position. These three chapters have no connection to the preceeding or succeeding text but is a subject so important in the mind of Paul, it cannot be left undocumented. These chapters are a complete work within themselves. We need not go to other books of the Bible to determine what Paul is saying in these three chapters.

Replacement theologians teach that Romans 9-11 refers to Spiritual Israel (the Church) and not to National Israel. Let us examine the Biblical text for the *literal* truth.

Paul immediately and proudly identifies himself as a Jew.

"For I could wish that myself were accursed from Christ for my brethren, my kinsmen *according to the flesh.*" (9:3)

The words "according to the flesh" could only speak of national Israel. Also, Paul would not need to feel a burden, as to wish he could be accursed for the church (Spiritual Israel). The burden for the church was born by Jesus Christ in the Garden of Gethsemane and at the Cross.

Eight-fold Identification of National Israel

That "His people" is national Israel and not the church is further supported by Paul's eight introductory statements that could only apply to national Israel.

The Mystery of Israel! / 121

"Who are Israelites, to whom pertain the adoption, the glory, the covenants, the giving of the law, the service of God, and the promises; of whom are the fathers and from whom, according to the flesh, Christ came ... (9:4-5)

1) *To whom pertain the adoption!* Israel is always represented in the Scripture as *God's first born son* among all people (Ex. 4:22 Deut. 14:1 Hosea 11:1). Not the Church, national Israel! Dr. H.L. Ellison states: "What concerns us at the moment is that *no evidence can be adduced that God disowned or disinherited His son Israel.* To this day Israel finds that the Law is his *paidagogos* (the slave responsible for taking the boy to school and seeing that he learnt his lessons), for he has not yet found his freedom in Christ (Gal.3:24), but the continuing work of the Law *testifies to his continuing sonship.*"

Simply stated, there is no way the integrity of God would permit Him to disinherit His first born son, natural Israel, for spiritual Israel (the church).

There are two supernatural births in Scripture ... Isaac and Jesus Christ. Isaac came from the womb "that was dead" and Jesus came from the womb of a virgin. Isaac is the genetic root of national Israel (9:7), Jesus is the spiritual root of the church.

2) *The glory* or the visible presence of the Shekinah (Ex. 24:16 Ezekiel 1:28 Hebrews 9:5). The Shekinah glory was the luminous cloud that led Israel out of Egypt's bondage, that rested over the Mercy Seat in the Holy of Holies, the visible manifestation of God's presence with His chosen people.

122 / *The Mystery of Israel!*

In the Christian mentality, the glory of God departed from the Synagogue, when Jesus left it. If the glory of God left the Synagogue why did Chrysostom denounce so viciously those Christians who were still attending the Synagogue three hundred years later? Why did Constantine enact a law making becoming a Jew a crime which was punishable by death? What was the attraction of the Synagogue to these Christians?

That Shekinah glory of national Israel is inscribed on every American one dollar bill, surrounding the thirteen stars of the Mogen David over the eagle's head. George Washington had it placed there as a lasting tribute to Haym Salomon and the Jewish people for their heroic part in the American Revolution.

3) *The covenants!* The only people God ever made a covenant with were the Jewish people, national Israel! There are fifteen different covenants in Scripture! Not one covenant was ever made with the Gentiles. God made these covenants with Israel because that nation was to be used as a channel to bring salvation to the world. For that reason, Jesus said, "Salvation is of the Jews."

The new covenant which Jesus announced at the last Supper, sealed on Golgatha and made effective at Pentecost, was at first confined to the Jewish people. The Church may experience the blessings of national Israel, but they never replace Israel in the economy of God. Israel's relationship to the covenant will be discussed later in the text.

4) *The giving of the Law!* Only national Israel received the Ten Commandments or the Law of God

The Mystery of Israel! / 123

as revealed through Moses. The Law was a continued revelation of God to man and it was a high honor God offered Israel in accepting the yoke of the Law.

The Law was not forced upon national Israel! They had free choice in the matter (Ex.19:8) and gladly chose to keep it. Christians criticize the Law while Moses praised the Law (Deut. 4:8). Christians interpret Paul's rejection of the Law for its powerlessness as rejection of its contents. Jesus said, "Do not think that I came to destroy the Law or the Prophets. I did not come to destroy but to fulfill" (Matthew 5:17).

5) *The service of God!* The service of God refers to the service as seen in the tabernacle, offerings, and priesthood as found in Exodus and Leviticus. The Jews, national Israel, were the only people who for 1500 years possessed the only form of worship designed and commanded by God Himself.

Those anti-Semitic theologians who trot about screeching that "Christianity is the only revelation of truth" are ignorant of both the Bible and history. Recognized Christianity is yet today pregnant with paganism!

Dr. Donald G. Barnhouse gives the following illustration. "When the great Jew, Disraeli, became Lord Beaconsfield, he was once twitted in the House of Lords because of his Jewish ancestry. With a courtly bow, he answered the seventeenth baron of something or other who had the bad taste to speak in such a fashion, and put him in his place forever. 'Yes, my nobel Lord,' replied Disraeli, 'I am a Jew. And when your ancestors were living on acorns in the German forest my ancestors were giving the world law, literature, religion and our very Saviour."

6) *The promises* of God! This refers to the Messianic promises which were given to national Israel (not spiritual Israel) that a Deliverer would come out of Zion. However much the nations rejoice in the riches they have found in Jesus Christ, they must never forget that they were first promised to Israel and through national Israel they have come. Not the Church!

7) *The fathers!* (9:5) The fathers (plural) are Abraham, Isaac and Jacob (Compare to Romans 11:28b). Spiritual Israel has one father which is in Heaven.

8) "and from whom, *according to the flesh,* Christ came ... " Christ's flesh and blood forefathers were Abraham, Isaac, Jacob and David (Matt 1:1) which could only speak of national Israel. Let us put to rest forever this myth that Jesus was not Jewish!

The Redeemed Remnant

There are two clearly defined groups of Jewish people in Romans nine through eleven. They are:
- The Redeemed Remnant according to the election of grace (9:11 9:27 11:5) and ...
- Those who are broken off from the olive tree under God's judgement and are in a state of partial blindness which is divinely caused (11:7 11:17 Deut. 29:4 Isaiah 29:10).

The Redeemed Remnant means that there are *right now* Jewish people on this earth who have a powerful

The Mystery of Israel! / 125

and special relationship with God. They have been chosen by the "election of grace" in which God does what he does without asking man to approve it or understand it. Let us put an end to this Christian chatter that *"all the Jews are lost"* and can't be in the will of God until they convert to Christianity!

What is the "election of grace?" God, throughout the ages, has had an exact purpose and plan for every man and nation. God is faithful to His purpose ... not to man's understanding of His purpose. We read in the Hebrew Covenant this theme of choice and rejection. Not Joseph, but Judah, not Shiloh but Zion (Psa. 78:60,67,68), not Saul but David.

Paul forcefully gives three illustrations in Romans nine to demonstrate God's "election of grace?"

1) Esau and Jacob (Romans 9:13)
2) Pharoah in Egypt (Romans 9:17)
3) The Potter and the clay (Romans 9:21)

Concerning Esau and Jacob, God who is all knowing, loved Jacob and hated Esau (9:13). It strains the mind of man to understand how God could make this decision when they were both yet in their mother's womb.

In this election of Jacob over Esau, God demonstrates that priority by natural claim does not weigh with Him. Esau was the first born and by *natural claim,* Jacob should have served him, yet he was the servant of Jacob. Jacob was elected by God *before* he was born, showing that nothing done by the elected one constitutes a claim on God's electing grace.

Christians who state, "The Jews don't deserve God's mercy" simply do not understand the doctrine of

election. The question might also be asked, "What did the Gentiles ever do to deserve God's mercy?" The sovereign God of Heaven has elected a remnant from among the Jews upon the earth as vessels of honor. Paul explains divine election 9:15 saying:
"For he (God) saith to Moses, I will have mercy upon whom I will have mercy, and I will have compassion on whom I will have compassion."
Concerning Pharoah in Egypt (9:17), Paul states that God raised Pharoah up so that God could demonstrate His power to all throughout the earth and that the name of Jehovah God would be declared as the true and living God. When Moses entered Pharoah's court from the backside of the desert and thundered, "Let my people go," Pharoah had an opportunity to choose between right and wrong. That opportunity was repeated ten times via ten plagues. He refused God's appeal for his opinion. God knew Pharoah would make that choice before Moses ever returned to in Egypt!

The Potter and the clay are more easily understood. The Potter refuses to explain his plan and purposes to the clay on his spinning wheel. It's easy to understand why the Potter would not enter into a dialogue of logic with the clay. It is not easy to understand how God would choose one man over another before birth.

Dr. Vincent gives added confirmation that these three chapters could *only refer to national Israel* by stating "the figure of man as clay molded by God (referring to Romans 9:21 with the Potter and the clay) carries us back to the earliest traditions of the creation of man." Man is created from the *dust* of the earth. His

The Mystery of Israel! / 127

flesh therefore is clay. That which is flesh is flesh and is national Israel and cannot be considered spiritual Israel.

There is no other logical conclusion based upon the Biblical text other than the fact that Romans nine speaks of national Israel and not the church and that there are a certain number of Jews in relationship with God right now through divine election.

How many are in that number? No one knows but we have Bible precedent that the number far exceeds our expectation. Elijah, a Jewish prophet, was suffering from severe depression. Tired and exhausted from his Charismatic Conference on the crest of Mt. Carmel and fearful of Jezebel's threat to murder him in cold blood the next day, he mounted the Pity Pot. "I have been very zealous for the Lord God Almighty. The Israelites have rejected your covenant, broken down your altars, and put your prophets to death with a sword. *I am the only one left,* and now they are trying to kill me" (I Kings 19:10).

Many Christians have "the only one left complex." Elijah, a godly Jewish prophet, in a state of fear and exhaustion, developed the idea that he was the only rightous Jew left on planet Earth. God told him to get off his Pity Pot because there were seven thousand righteous Jews in that area who had not bowed their knee to Baal.

The point is, Elijah, being Jewish, should have known about those 7000 righteous Jews. He did not know them but they were known to God. Just as there was a remnant then not known to Elijah, there is a remnant now not known to the Gentile Church but known and loved of God!

Paul completes chapter nine by saying; "Except the Lord of Sabbath had *left us a seed,* we had been as Sodom and Gomorrha." (9:29) Sodom and Gomorrah were the two wicked homosexual cities God absolutely destroyed with fire and brimstone after evacuating most of Lot's family. Some scholars think that the twin cities are located under the Dead Sea which is the reason that sea has such a sulphric taste to the water caused by the brimstone. It was so totally destroyed not a shred of it has been found to this date.

Paul states that unless God had *left a seed* (for national Israel to be re-born), national Israel would have been destroyed like Sodom and Gomorrah. There is no way this could apply to the Church.

Romans Eleven Rebutts Replacement Theology!

Paul opens Romans chapter eleven with:
"I say then, has God cast away His people? *Certainly not!* For I also am an Israelite, of the seed of Abraham, of the tribe of Benjamin (11:1).
Dr. Kenneth S. Wuest says, "The question is so phrased in the Greek text that it requires a negative answer. Paul is not raising a question. He is driving home the fact that God did not cast away Israel. He uses the rhetorical question, "God did not cast away His people, did he?" It is obvious that 'his people' must mean the people of God *nationally* considered. Thus the

covenant of God with Israel, having been national, shall ultimately be fulfilled in them as a nation." The question of replacement is so strong upon Paul's mind that he brings it up again in verse eleven: "I say then, have they stumbled that they should fall? *Certainly not!* ... "

The Three Branches

The Jewish people and Judaism, as taught by Moses, have a living relationship with God right now. Notice in the reading of Romans chapter eleven, the fact that the olive tree in scripture is characteristic of national Israel (Psalm 52:8 Jeremiah 11:16 Hosea 14:6) and that there are three kinds of branches mentioned.

"And if *some of the branches* were broken off, and you being a wild olive tree, were *grafted in* among them, and with them became a partaker of the root and the fatness of the olive tree."

The three branches are:

1) Natural branches (Jews) cut off for disobedience to God. (Romans 11:19 see also Isaiah 65:2-5 Deut. 28:15,25,63,67 and Ezekiel 6:4-10).

2) Natural branches (Jews) *still growing* on the root. "And if *some of the branches* were broken off ... " Some of the branches is not *all* of the branches. Some are broken off ... some are still on the tree.

3) And wild olive branches (Gentile Christians) grafted into the root (Romans 11:17).

Note that the Jewish roots of national Israel (11:18) support spiritual Israel. Paul sternly warns Gentile

Christians about the arrogant spirit of Replacement Theology with... "do not boast against the branches." (Jews who are under God's discipline) If you do, God will not spare you. (11:20-21)

Judaism does not need Christianity to explain its existence. Yet, Christianity must have Judaism, as taught by Moses, to explain our existence. If Christians want to bear fruit as grafted in branches, they are commanded to "remember the root." Simply stated, *to bear fruit, remember the root.*

CHAPTER NINE
JUST HOW JEWISH WAS JESUS?

It is essential for Replacement theologians and other anti-Semites to separate Jesus from His Jewish roots. Why? If you can separate Jesus from the Jewish people, hatred becomes fashionable and anti-Semitism becomes a Christian virtue. An anti-Semite is a dead Christian whose hatred has strangled his faith. Like a chameleon, anti-Semitism can masquerade alternately as "doing the will of God" or political ideology.

If Jesus can be separated from His Jewish roots, Christians can continue to praise the dead Jews of the past (Abraham, Isaac and Jacob) while hating the Goldberg's across the street. When you see the Jewish people as the family of our Lord, they become our extended family whom we are commanded to love unconditionally.

Adolf Hitler knew he must destroy the Jewish roots of Jesus in the minds of the German people. His demented mind created the Mischlinge Regulation which defined a Jew as someone with two Jewish parents. He did this for two reasons. One, he must absolve Jesus of being Jewish or his Nazi goons would never enthusiastically murder six million of His relatives. Secondly, Hitler feared he was partly Jewish.

John Toland, Pulitzer Prize winning historian, records in his book, *Adolf Hitler,* that Hitler's father's birth certificate declared him to be "illegitimate." The

132 / *Just How Jewish Was Jesus?*

space for the father's name on the birth certificate was left blank, generating a mystery that remains unsolved.

There is a distinct possibility that Hitler's grandfather was a wealthy Jew named Frankenberger or Frankenreither. Hitler was so concerned about the matter that he ordered his personal attorney, Hans Frank, to investigate the matter confidentially. Hans' report, gathered from "all possible sources," greatly disturbed Hitler. Frank's report concluded regretfully, the possibility could not be dismissed that Hitler's father was half-Jewish. If true, Hitler would fit the historical pattern of half-Jews that have tormented the Jewish people from the beginning of time.

The Mischlinge Regulation separated Hitler from his Jewish past and Jesus from the Jews of Germany. (Because of Mary's immaculate conception, Jesus had just one Jewish parent). Hitler made Jew hating "the will of God." Replacement theologians are now carrying Hitler's anointing and his message! Hitler wrote in *Mein Kampf,*

"Hence today I believe that I am acting in accordance with the will of the Almighty Creator: by defending myself against the Jew, I am fighting for the *work of the Lord.*"

Most Christians think of Jesus and His disciples as Christians before their time. Not so! Jesus was not a Christian! He was born to Jewish parents, He was dedicated in the Jewish tradition, He was reared studying the words of Moses and the prophets of Israel, He became a Jewish Rabbi and He died with a sign over

Just How Jewish Was Jesus? / 133

his head written in three languages, "This is the King of the Jews!"

Jesus died without ever hearing the word "Christian." The word was used for the first time in Antioch, forty years after His crucifixion (Acts 11:26). The word was used by the heathen to describe the loving conduct of those who followed the teachings of this gentle Jewish Rabbi. One wonders what word would be coined today, by the heathen, to describe Christian conduct one toward the other.

If Jesus Christ came to your church this Sunday morning, would the ushers let him enter the front door? He would appear small and slender with penetrating dark eyes, a swarthy complexion and prominent Semitic features. He would have the long falling earlocks of the Hebrews, his hair uncut at the corners, a full manly beard and his shoulders draped with a Tallit (Prayer Shawl) whose message yet remains a mystery to Christianity.

If Jesus identified Himself to your congregation as a Jewish Rabbi who befriended a prostitute, socialized with tax collectors and other social outcasts, who was hated by the government and was surrounded with twelve, full bearded, unemployed men with shoulder length hair, could they get a seat? Probably not!

If He was asked by your deacons about His doctrinal positions and He responded, "I believe in baptism by immersion, casting out demons, healing the sick and speaking in new tongues" (Mark 17:17-18), would they let him in the pulpit? Not hardly!

134 / *Just How Jewish Was Jesus?*

If He commanded your wealthiest church members to sell all they had to give to the poor, or He entered your beautiful church gym and turned over the bingo tables, shouting, "My house shall be called a house of prayer," (Luke 19:46), would they call the police? Absolutely! The simple truth is, after two thousand years of anti-Semitic teaching and preaching, we have lost sight of our Hebrew Lord. Just how Jewish was Jesus?

His Parents were Jewish!

Jesus of Nazareth was of the tribe of Judah linked to David, Abraham, and Moses (Matthew 1:1-2). His name, Jesus Christ, was given to Mary by God's angel. Jesus was his given name and is the Greek form of Joshua which means the Lord saves. Christ was the name that labeled Him as the "Anointed One."

But His last name was Goldberg, or Rosenberg, or perhaps Scheinberg. I can assure you that Mary and Joseph were not carried on the Roman Tax Rolls as

Mr. and Mrs. Christ
One Cave Lane
Bethlehem, Palestine

Mary and Joseph raised Jesus in the Jewish manner of life. He was taken to the Temple to be circumcised on the eighth day by the High Priest Simeon which was and is a very Jewish event (Luke 2:39).

At the end of His twelfth year, which would have been his thirteenth birthday, Jesus was taken to the Temple for His Bar Mitzvah, which was and is the custom of the Jews (Luke 2:42). The Bar Mitzvah is the

Just How Jewish Was Jesus? / 135

point in life when a Jewish boy becomes a man. Jesus went into the Temple a boy, he came out of the Temple a man.

In that context, it is not hard to understand the controversial conversation between Jesus and His mother following His Bar Mitzvah. When Mary and Joseph left the Temple and discovered after one day's journey that Jesus was not with them, they returned to the Temple to find their son in a dialogue with scholars. Mary scolded Jesus, saying,

"Son, why have you done this to us? Your father and I have sought you anxiously." Jesus answered, "Why is it that you sought me?" (Luke 2:48-49)

Christians see Jesus' response as being disrespectful to His mother. He was not! Jesus was now a man and His Jewish mother was having difficulty adjusting to the fact. There are some things that never change!

Many Christian teachers say, "We know nothing about the life of Jesus from His twelfth year until His public ministry began at age thirty." Not so! Because Jesus was Jewish we know what He was doing at every phase of His life. From *Everyman's Talmud* we read:

"At five years, the age is reached for the study of scripture; at ten, for the study of Mishnah; at thirteen, for the fulfillment of the commandments (Bar Mitzvah); at fifteen, for the study of Talmud, at eighteen, for marriage; at twenty for seeking livelihood; at thirty, for entering into one's full strength (life's work)."

Jesus, therefore, began studying the scripture at the age of five; he studied the Mishnah at the age of ten and was Bar Mitzvahed at age thirteen in the Temple. At fifteen, He studied the Talmud; knowing the Cross was before Him, he did not marry at eighteen; at twenty, He worked as a carpenter with His father Joseph and began His public ministry at age thirty, having reached His full strength.

Jesus Practiced Traditional Judaism

Those who say that Jesus did not practice traditional Judaism have no knowledge of history or Scripture. The fact is, the only faith on the face of the earth during the life of Jesus that believed in a single omnipotent Supreme Being was Judaism. The only theology that God ever created was Judaism! It was the lone voice of Judaism that shouted to a pagan world saturated with polytheistic deities, "Hear, O Israel, the Lord our God is One."

It was Judaism that believed man was created in God's image. It was traditional Judaism that gave us the concepts of hell, heaven, angels, devils, the acceptance of Adam and Eve as the first man and woman, the creation of the world in seven days, and even its age, four thousand years.

It was Judaism that taught us to sing while other religions wail in sorrow. It was Judaism that gave us love and respect for life. While pagan religions sacrificed their children to foreign gods, Judaism gave us a loving God who adored the life of every child.

Just How Jewish Was Jesus? / 137

It was Judaism that gave us the Lord's Supper, which is a part of the Passover celebration, commemorating the breaking of bread and taking the communion cup. Early Christians celebrated the Passover for three hundred years after the death of Jesus until Constantine made it illegal, in an effort to separate Jews from Gentiles.

It was Judaism that gave us the patriarchs, the prophets, the Scripture and our Hebrew Lord. For that reason, Rabbi Jesus of Nazareth said, "Salvation is of the Jews" (John 4:22). Every word of the New Testament verifies that Jesus, his family and his disciples practiced traditional Judaism every day of their lives.

Jesus Wore a Tallit

The Tallit (Prayer Shawl) is a mystery to Christians even though we've read about it in the Scripture all of our lives. Its powerful spiritual message is hidden because we have lost contact with our Jewish roots.

The Tallit (pronounced ta-leet) is a garment designed by God Himself. God commanded Moses to tell all the men of Israel that they were to wear the Prayer Shawl forever.

"The Lord said to Moses, "Speak to the Israelites and say to them: Throughout the *generations to come* you are to make tassels on the corners of your garments, with a blue cord on each tassel. You will have these tassels to look at so *you will remember* all the commandments of the Lord, that *you may obey* them and not prostitute yourselves by going

138 / *Just How Jewish Was Jesus?*

after the lust of your own hearts and eyes. Then you shall remember to obey all my commandments and *will be consecrated* to your God" (Numbers 15:37-40 NIV).

Jesus Christ was part of the "generations to come." He wore a Prayer Shawl in obedience to the will of the Father. That Prayer Shawl was with him every day of His public ministry and went with Him into His grave. Archaeologists have uncovered Prayer Shawls that date back to the second century.

(Artist rendering of the Prayer Shawl)

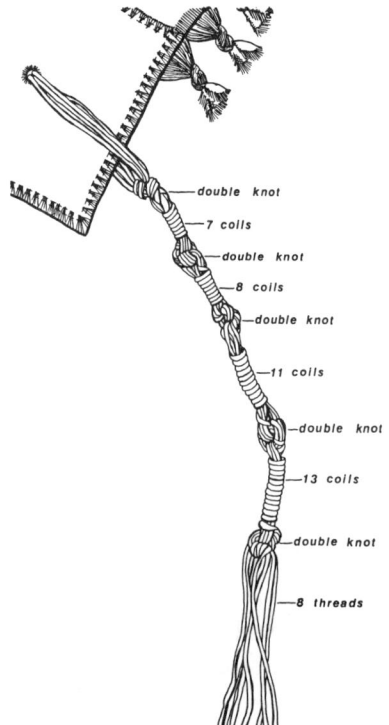

The Tallit is rectangular and looks like a tent with a guy rope in each corner. The guy ropes are called tzitzit. The Shawl has tassels on two edges and a ribbon of blue running the length of the garment on both sides. The tassels and the tzitzit, represent the 613 commandments of the Torah (first five books of the Bible) that righteous Jews obey. Each time the men of Israel put on their Prayer Shawls, they were reminded of the Word of God, they were reminded of the will of God, they were encouraged to obey God and to be consecrated unto Him. Each time they placed this divinely designed garment about their shoulders, they were reminded that God lived in the blue heavens, not on earth as did Egyptian gods. The blue band running the length of the garment spoke of heaven. When the Jews entered the Tabernacle, the first flap they saw was blue. The Prayer Shawl was in fact every man's portable tabernacle. The Prayer Shawl also identified the name of Jehovah God.

The Tallit Identifies Jehovah

In the four corners of the Tallit, we see a unique series of coils and knots called the tzitzit which spell out the letters that identify the God of Israel as Jehovah. In the Hebrew language, letters of the alphabet have numerical value. This is scripturally verified by the writings of John who said in the Revelation that the coming Anti-Christ could be identified by calculating the numerology of his name. John writes, "This calls

for wisdom. If anyone has insight, let him calculate the number of the beast, for it is a man's number. His number is 666." (Rev.13:18 NIV)
Remember that the children of Israel were coming out of four hundred years of captivity in a polytheistic society. God had physically removed them from Egypt in the miracle of Passover, now He was trying to spiritually remove Egypt out of them. He began by announcing that there was only one God, not a pantheon of gods.
"Hear O Israel, The Lord our God is one Lord." Deut. 6:4
God continued telling the Chosen People who He was because they did not know Him as Jehovah God, the only true God.
"And I appeared unto Abraham, unto Isaac and unto Jacob, by the name of God Almighty, but by my name Jehovah was *I not known* unto them" Exodus 6:4.
God, through Hebrew numerology, uses the tzitzit in the four corners of the Prayer Shawl to identify who He is to the Jewish people forever. The tzitzit begins with seven coils, a double knot, followed by eight coils. Seven and eight equal fifteen, a number made up of 10 and 5. In Hebrew numerology 10 = the letter Yud and 5 = the letter Heh.
After these fifteen coils comes another double knot followed by eleven coils. The number eleven is made up of the numbers 6 and 5 which represent the Hebrew letters Vav and Heh. Putting all these letters together, we have Yud-Heh-Vav-Heh (YHVH) which means

Just How Jewish Was Jesus? / 141

Jehovah God. Each time Jesus put on His Prayer Shawl, He was reminded of His Father in heaven. Each time a Jewish man, from Moses until today, puts on his Prayer Shawl, he is reminded that there is One God in Israel.

The Prayer Closet

What did Jesus mean when He said, "But when thou prayest, enter into *thy closet* (secret chamber)... and thy father which seeth in secret shall reward thee openly" (Matt. 6:6). The mystery of the meaning is revealed in the Prayer Shawl.

As the Jewish man reaches for his Prayer Shawl to pray, he kisses the edge of it for it is sacred and dearly loved. It reminds him of the Torah which is the Word of God, it reminds him of the will of God, it reminds him of the place where God lives and the name of God. While Christians have been led to believe that the Law of God was grievous, the Biblical text states exactly the opposite. King David said, "But *his delight* is in the law of the Lord, and on his law he meditates day and night" (Psalm 1:2).

After kissing the sacred Shawl, the Jewish man takes it by two corners and stretches it over his head making a tent, or tabernacle, as he quotes Psalm 104:1-2:

"Praise the Lord, O my soul. O Lord my God, you are very great, you are clothed with splendor and majesty, he wraps himself in light as with a garment, he stretches out the heavens *like a tent*."

After entering into the courts of God with thanksgiving and praise, it is now time to enter into the prayer closet, or secret chamber, where he will talk to God about the innermost feelings of his heart. It is too personal for others to hear. By simply folding his hands downward, the Jewish man is enveloped in his personal prayer closet. He is in the secret chamber of his personal tabernacle.

When the Prophet Balaam looked down from the mountain where he was supposed to curse Israel, he saw Israel camped in the valley below and said:

"How beautiful are *thy tents,* O Jacob, and thy tabernacles, O Israel." (Numbers 24:5)

What was Balaam seeing? He saw the men of Israel, standing row upon row, with their Prayer Shawls covering their heads like tents, praying and worshiping the living God of Israel. Balaam confessed, "The shout of a King is among them."

The Tallit in Prophecy

The Prayer Shawl in Prophecy? Yes! The Prophet Isaiah said:

"He (God) will raise a banner (flag) for the nations and gather the exiles of Israel." Isaiah 11:12

The "exiles of Israel" are the Jews who were scattered to the four winds of the earth and were buried in Gentile graves during the Diaspora. God said through the Prophet Isaiah, He had designed a flag and under that banner, the Jews of the world would return to the

Just How Jewish Was Jesus? / 143

Jewish State. The miracle of miracles became reality, May 15, 1948 when Israel was reborn in a day (Isa. 66:8).

Under what flag did they gather? They gathered under a flag designed in the chambers of heaven with borders of blue. If you take the Prayer Shawl and attach a Star of David in the center between the borders of blue, you have the flag of Israel. It waves proudly over a free and independent Jewish State, by the will of God.

The Tallit in Jesus' Ministry

The Tallit was worn by Jesus every day of His adult life. How do we know that? When He stood before His Jewish audience, who knew the Law of God as given through Moses verbatim, He said, "Which one of you convinceth me of sin?" (John 8:46). If Jesus had not been wearing His Prayer Shawl, every Jewish man listening would have immediately reminded Him of God's command to wear the Shawl.

The Prayer Shawl was a dramatic point of contact in the healing ministry of Jesus. As He walked down the grassy lanes of Israel, people reached to touch the hem of His garment. They were reaching for the fringes of His Prayer Shawl.

"And a certain woman, which had an issue of blood twelve year, And had suffered many things of many physicians ... when she heard of Jesus, came in the press behind, and touched his garment. For she said, If I may touch but his clothes

144 / *Just How Jewish Was Jesus?*

(Prayer Shawl), I shall be whole. And straightway the fountain of her blood was dried up; and she felt in her body that she was healed of the plague." (Mark 5:25-30)

Jesus was on His way to pray for the twelve year old daughter of Jairus, who was dying with a raging fever. En route to the house of Jairus, the woman with the issue of blood reached out and touched the tzitzit, or fringe on the hem of Jesus' Tallit.

The word "hem" in the Greek is "kraspedon" meaning a "tassel of twisted wool." The woman was reaching for the tassels of Jesus' Prayer Shawl, not his Haggar slacks. The woman was healed instantly when she touched the Shawl.

Messengers came from the house of Jairus and said the twelve year old girl was dead. Jesus entered the home and placed His Tallit over the body of the girl and bound her hands as Elijah had done in raising the son of the widow of Nain. Jesus spoke to the dead girl, saying: "Talitha cumi." The monks placed their interpretation of his words in parenthesis... (which is, being interpreted, Damsel, I say unto thee arise.")

"Talitha cumi" does not mean, "Damsel, I say unto thee arise." Had Jesus addressed her as a twelve year old girl, the Hebrew phrase would have been "yaldah cumi." Had she been thirteen to seventeen years of age, Jesus would have said "Almah cumi" meaning "teenage girl arise." Had she been eighteen or over, and unmarried, he would have said, "Betulah cumi" or "Miss, stand up!"

Just How Jewish Was Jesus? / 145

The word "talLieYTahH" means "she which is in the Tallit or Prayer Shawl" and "QouMi" is Hebrew feminine imperative for "arise." She was raised from the dead and countless others were healed as they touched the Prayer Shawl of Jesus.

"And withersoever he entered, into villages or cities, or country, they laid the sick in the streets, and besought that they might touch if it were but the *border of his garment*: and as many as touched him were made whole." (Mark 6:56)

Tallit in the Resurrection

The Prayer Shawl was such a sacred and personal item many Jewish men were buried with their Shawl. The Shawl was often wrapped around the head of the deceased as did Lazarus in John 11:44. Jesus went to the tomb with His Prayer Shawl and it became the ultimate verification of His resurrection.

A seldom recognized verse of Scripture in the Gospel of John tells the story of the events of the resurrection morning.

"Then cometh Simon Peter following him, and went into the sepulcher, and seeth linen clothes lie, *And the napkin,* that was about his head, not lying with the linen clothes, but wrapped together in a place by itself." (John 20:6-7)

The "napkin" was the Prayer Shawl of Jesus!

When Simon Peter burst into the empty tomb, he found the Prayer Shawl not with the other grave clothes but "wrapped together" (neatly folded) in a place by itself. The Jews have an exact and precise manner for folding the Prayer Shawl just as the American military precisely folds the U.S. flag. Jesus knew that when Simon Peter burst into the empty tomb and could not find His body, Peter would think the Romans had stolen the body of Christ. Therefore, Jesus took the time on the morning of His resurrection to precisely fold the Prayer Shawl and lay it conspicuously away from the other grave clothes.

When Peter saw the neatly folded Prayer Shawl, he knew the Romans had not stolen the body of Jesus. You have to be alive to fold the Shawl and you have to be Jewish to know how. The only one in the tomb was Jesus. The folded Prayer Shawl triumphantly announced to His disciples, "He's alive!"

The Tallit In His Return

Jesus Christ of Nazareth is coming back! When He returns, He will not come to Rome, He will not come to Washington D.C., He will come to Jerusalem as the Lion of the tribe of Judah and as the eternal heir to the throne of King David. He will usher in the Perfect Age where men will study war no more and the Lion will lay down with the Lamb. Some theologians are teaching that we are in the millennium now. If you believe that, throw a lamb in a lion's cage and see what happens.

Just How Jewish Was Jesus? / 147

Jesus left this earth as a Jewish Rabbi and will return as a Jewish Rabbi (Acts 1:11) wearing His Prayer Shawl. John the Revelator describes His return:
> "And I saw heaven opened, and behold a white horse; and he that sat upon him was called Faithful and True, and in righteousness he doth judge and make war. His eyes were as a flame of fire, and on his head were many crowns; and he had a name written that *no man knew but he himself.* And he was clothed with a *vesture dipped in blood:* and his name was called the Word of God. And the armies which were in heaven followed him upon white horses, clothed in fine linen, white and clean. And he hath on his vesture and on his thigh a name written, KING OF KINGS AND LORD OF LORDS" (Revelation 19:11-16).

John describes the return of Jesus Christ as He is descending from heaven mounted on a white horse. He comes as a mighty conqueror to judge the earth with a rod of iron and to make war on the enemies of Israel. The "armies which were in heaven" will fight with Christ against those nations which are attacking Israel until those nations are annihilated.

John writes, "he had a name written that no man knew but he himself." As a Jew, John remembers that God appeared unto Abraham, Isaac and Jacob by the name of God Almighty, but by the name of Jehovah *he was not known* unto them (Exodus 6:3).

John then describes a vesture dipped in blood. Many teach that this is the blood of those that are slain in this

final war. How could it be? Jesus in this scripture is seen by John as being in the heavens (Rev. 19:11) and his enemies are on the ground. Therefore the blood on His clothes cannot be the blood of His enemies. Whose blood is it? It's His blood which was shed in His warfare with Satan on the Cross. And what is this vesture? It is His Prayer Shawl! Scriptural evidence supporting this fact is recorded by John:
> "And he hath on his vesture and on his thigh a name written, KING OF KINGS AND LORD OF LORDS" (Rev. 19:16).

How can a name be written on a man's thigh? When I was a child, I heard an evangelist in my father's church refer to the "tattoo on Jesus thigh." Logic will tell you that if it were written on His actual thigh by any method, it would be covered by His outer garments.

How did John the Revelator see the name of Jesus on His thigh? John saw Jesus returning to earth riding the white horse of a mighty conqueror wearing His Prayer Shawl. The name of Jehovah God is spelled out in each of the four corners with the unique coils and knots of the tzitzit. When sitting upon a horse, the four tzitzits of the Prayer Shawl hit you exactly on the thigh.

The preponderance of Scriptural evidence is staggering establishing the Jewishness of Jesus. He was born to Jewish parents, His ancestors were Jewish, He was raised in the Jewish tradition, He lived and worshiped as a Jew, He died as a Jew and will return as a Jew. When you kneel tonight to pray, the One who hears you is a Jewish Rabbi named Jesus of Nazareth.

CHAPTER TEN
"AND IN THEE SHALL ALL NATIONS BE BLESSED"

The Jewish people have indeed blessed all the nations of the earth. The contributions of the Jewish people is staggering considering their minuscule number. Mark Twain said of the Jewish people, "If the statistics are right, the Jews constitute but one quarter of one percent of the human race. It suggests a nebulous dim puff of stardust lost in the blaze of the Milky Way. Properly, the Jew ought hardly to be heard of; but he is heard of, has always been heard of. He is as prominent on the planet as any other people, and his importance is extravagantly out of proportion to the smallness of his bulk.

"His contributions to the world's list of great names in literature, science, art, music, finance, medicine and abstruse learning are very out of proportion to the weakness of his numbers. He has made a marvelous fight in this world in all ages; and has done it with his hands tied behind him. He could be vain of himself and be excused for it. The Egyptians, the Babylonians and the Persians rose, filled the planet with sound and splendor; then faded to dream-stuff and passed away; the Greeks and the Romans followed and made a vast noise, and they are gone; other people have sprung up and held their torch high for a time but it burned out, and they sit in twilight now, or have vanished.

150 / "And In Thee Shall All Nations Be Blessed"

"The Jews saw them all, survived them all, and is now what he always was, exhibiting no decadence, no infirmities of age, no weakening of his parts, no slowing of his energies, no dulling of his alert and aggressive mind. All things are mortal but the Jew; all other forces pass, but he remains. What is the secret of his immortality?"

The secret of Jewish immortality lies in the supernatural! Jehovah God created the Jewish nation with His spoken word:

"Now the Lord said to Abram, 'Get out of your country, from your kindred and from your father's house, *to a land* that I will show you. I will make you a great nation; I will bless you and make your name great; and you shall be a blessing. *I will bless those who bless you* and *curse those who curse you*; and in you shall *all the families of the earth* be blessed." (Gen. 12:1-3)

Three chapters later, God Himself entered into an elaborate blood covenant with Abraham, transferring the clear and unclouded Title Deed of Israel to his heirs through Isaac and Jacob forever. (Gen. 15:9-21). He created the nation of Israel, He designed the flag of the nation of Israel, He has chosen Israel as His habitation and has sworn to defend Israel.

"Behold, he that keepeth Israel shall neither slumber nor sleep!" (Psa. 121:4) "They that trust in the Lord shall be as mount Zion, which *cannot be removed but abideth forever.* As the mountains are round about Jerusalem, so the Lord is round

"And In Thee Shall All Nations Be Blessed" / 151

about his people (the Jews) from henceforth *even for ever."* (Psa. 125:1-2)

The Bible and World History testify that the Jewish people have blessed the nations of the earth and those nations have tried diligently to ignore those contributions.

God Blesses The Gentiles Through The Jews

Shakespeare's pen created the greedy, money-hungry "Shylock" and the image of the deceitful business man has ever haunted the Jewish people. There is a Shylock in the book of Genesis; his name is Laban ... and he's a Gentile!

Laban was the Syrian father-in-law of Jacob who abused Jacob by changing his wages ten times, each time to Jacob's hurt. He also tricked Jacob into working fourteen years for the hand of his daughter, Rachel. Laban, in the Biblical text, is a deceitful, fraudulent, and untrustworthy employer.

After more than fourteen years of abuse, Jacob, the employee, comes to Laban, the employer, and submits his resignation. The words that Laban spoke when he knew that he was about to lose Jacob as an employee, reveals a divine truth that yet remains upon the earth. That truth is God blesses the Gentiles through the Jewish people.

"And Laban said unto him (Jacob), 'Please stay, if I have found favor in your eyes, for I have learned by experience that the Lord has *blessed me for your sake"* (Gen. 30:27).

"And In Thee Shall All Nations Be Blessed"

The next prominent Gentiles to learn the principle that God blesses the Gentiles through the Jewish people were Potiphar and Pharoah. Joseph was the Jewish Ambassador, send by God into Egypt, to bless the Gentiles and to preserve the nations of the world.

One Jewish boy went down into Egypt in chains by camel caravan, having been sold by his ten jealous elder brothers to Midianite merchants passing through Canaan. He was sold for twenty shekels of silver.

When the merchants arrived in Egypt, Joseph was sold a second time on the open slave market to an Egyptian official named Potiphar, the captain of Pharoah's guard.

The Lord was with Joseph and gave him absolute success as the business manager of Potiphar's vast estate. It is recorded in the Scripture:

" ... the Lord blessed the Egyptian's house *for Joseph's sake;* and the blessing of the Lord was upon all that he had in the house, and in the field" (Gen. 39:5).

In the process of time, Pharoah appointed Joseph as the Prime Minister of Egypt with these words, "Can we find another man like this man, one in whom is the Spirit of God? Since God has made all this known unto you, there is no one so discerning and wise as you. You are in charge of my palace, and all the people of Egypt will submit to your orders. Only with respect to the throne will I be greater than you."

Pharoah put the massive gold signet ring, bearing the kings name and seal, on Joseph finger, authorizing him to transact all of Pharoah's official business.

"And In Thee Shall All Nations Be Blessed"

Joseph was dressed in royal robes of fine linen and the golden chain of the Prime Minister's office was placed about his neck. He rode in Pharoah's chariot with men running before him shouting, "Make way! Make way!" Pharoah said to Joseph, "I am Pharoah, but without your word, no one can lift a hand or foot in all of Egypt."

The teenage slave of yesterday had become today's thirty year old Prime Minister of Egypt, the wealthiest and mightiest civilization on the face of the earth. Yesterday Joseph came into Egypt with chains of iron about his neck, today there were chains of gold. Yesterday a prisoner, today Prime Minister. Yesterday, he rode the backs of mangy camels into a slave market; today, he rode in a royal chariot pulled by matching prancing stallions with heralds running before him, announcing the coming of Egypt's most honored citizen.

When the seven years of famine came that Joseph had predicted and the world ran out of food, Joseph, the Jewish Ambassador, bartered with the nations of the earth until Egypt literally controlled the known world. As long as Pharaoh blessed Joseph and the Jews, Egypt's prosperity was so staggering, world historians struggle to accurately describe its splendor.

Egypt became the envy of the world. No nation on earth had a fraction of her wealth, military power or dazzling architectural beauty. Egypt prospered in personal health, international finance and agricultural accomplishment. "In thee shall all the nations of the earth be blessed."

154 / "And In Thee Shall All Nations Be Blessed"

The Bible principle that the Gentiles are blessed through the Jewish people is verified in the New Testament. Jesus Christ of Nazareth, a Rabbi, was " a light to bring revelation to the Gentiles ... "(Luke 2:32)

When the Samaritan woman (a Gentile) went to the well to get water, Jesus said to her, "You (Gentiles) worship what you do not know; we (the Jews) know what we worship, for salvation is of the Jews" (John 4:22).

It was the Jewish people who brought the light of God and salvation to the Gentiles. The patriarchs were Jewish, the prophets were Jewish, and Jesus of Nazareth was Jewish. How much salvation would there be without the Jewish people?

Every word of The HOLY BIBLE was written by the Jewish people. It is the light of truth and reason upon which our society and civilization is built.

George Washington said, "It is impossible to rightly govern the world without the Bible."

Abraham Lincoln said, "I believe the Bible is the best gift God has ever given to man. All the good from the Savior of the world is communicated to us through this book."

Napoleon said, "The Bible is no mere book, but a Living Creature, with a power that conquers all that oppose it."

Daniel Webster said, "If there is anything in my thoughts or style to command, the credit is due my parents for instilling in me an early love of the Scriptures. If we abide by the principles taught in the Bible, our country will go on prospering and to prosper;

"And In Thee Shall All Nations Be Blessed" / 155

but if we in our prosperity neglect its instructions and authority, no man can tell how sudden a catastrophe may overwhelm us and bury all our glory in profound obscurity."

Benjamin Disraeli, Earl of Baconsfield, (1804-1881), who was a Jewish British statesman and novelist, was being assaulted in the House of Commons for his Jewishness by an anti-Semite. Disraeli responded to his attacker with, "Yes, while your ancestors were rooting for acorns in the forest and sleeping in caves, my ancestors were giving the world the light of reason, literature, poetry and the foundations of civilizations."

Before the genius of Steven Spielberg gave us "E.T.," the pen of Isaiah and Jeremiah recorded the story of Elijah being transported from earth in a space vehicle in the original "Chariot of Fire" (2 Kings 2:11).

Before the movie JAWS emptied the beaches of the world with its celloid terrorism, the pen of Jonah recorded how he was swallowed alive by a "great fish" and was three days and nights in its stomach before being vomited out on dry land. Now that's a fish story!

Before our minds were tickled with the concept of talking to supernatural personalities in "Close Encounters of a Third Kind," there was Moses talking to God in person on Mt. Sinai.

The HOLY BIBLE is a book of poetry, history, love, sex, romance, war, adventure and an introduction to the living God of Heaven. Every chapter, every line and every word was penned by Jewish hands. "In thee shall all the nations of the earth be blessed."

The Jewish Contribution to America

In 1492, King Ferdinand and Queen Isabella of Spain signed the Edict of Expulsion, demanding that the Jews of Spain convert to Christianity or be expelled from Spain. The Jewish people were forced again in history to look for a new home. That search began as Jewish businessmen funded a Marrano (Jewish person pretending to be Catholic to avoid persecution from the Church of Rome) sailor named Christopher Columbus.

Columbus began the account of his voyage to the new world with a reference to the expulsion of the Jews from Spain. In one document he refers to the Second Temple in Jerusalem by the Hebraic term "Second House" that he dates as the year '68 in accordance with Jewish tradition. Columbus seems to have deliberately delayed the day of his sailing until August 3 so he would not be sailing on the Ninth of Av which is the day of the destruction of the Temple.

As Spain closed its doors to the Jews, ending five hundred years of the Golden Era, a new world was opening its doors to what would in time become America. The hands that pulled the door open were Jewish. "In thee shall all the nations of the earth be blessed."

The American Revolution

During the American Revolution, when it appeared George Washington and his forces were going to be defeated by Great Britain because of the lack of food, arms and ammunition, the financial hero of the

"And In Thee Shall All Nations Be Blessed" / 157

American Revolution, Haym Salomon, and the Jews of the thirteen colonies responded with massive financial aid that turned the tide of battle.

Salomon, a Philadelphia banker, went to George Washington at the beginning of the revolution and offered him his entire fortune of 600,000 pounds in British sterling to the war effort. As the Revolutionary war progressed and Washington's army was in dire need, Salomon went to Europe and met with business associates, the Sassoons and Rothchilds. They raised an additional three and one half million British sterling, or its equivalent, to turn the tide of battle that birthed America's freedom.

George Washington was so grateful to the Jewish people for their generous contribution to the American Revolution that he ordered the engravers of the American one dollar bill to inscribe a permanent tribute to them. If the reader will examine a one dollar bill, he will discover that immediately over the head of the American eagle is the Star of David with its distinctive thirteen star cluster. Surrounding the Star of David is the brilliant light of the Shekinah Glory that dwelt above the Mercy Seat in the Holy of Holies in the Jewish Tabernacle.

If you turn your one dollar bill upside down and place your thumb over the eagle's head, the shield becomes the menorah or the seven golden candlesticks of Israel. Placing your thumb over the shield completely leaves the tail of nine feathers which represents the flames of the Hanukkah Menorah.

158 / *"And In Thee Shall All Nations Be Blessed"*

The number thirteen to the Israelites is a perfect number. There were thirteen tribes including the Levites, a boy becomes a man at thirteen, and a girl becomes a woman at thirteen. There are thirteen leaves in the olive branch in the right talon of the eagle, thirteen arrows in the left, thirteen stripes on the shield, thirteen stars in the cloud representing the thirteen colonies. The Jewish contribution to the American Revolution is staggering. Every American who carries a one dollar bill has a constant reminder that "in thee shall all the nations of the earth be blessed."
Haym Salomon died in his middle forties penniless! He gave his fortune toward the birth of America without a legal note and without asking for interest to be paid to his heirs by the infant republic. America has never repaid that debt.

Chaim Weitzmann — WW I

During the First World War, when the prospect of an Allied victory was dim, when freedom in the western world was hanging by a thread, when the British navy ruled the seas but were running short of gun powder, the First Lord of the Admiralty, Sir Winston Churchill, contacted a brilliant Jewish chemist for help. His name was Chaim Weitzmann.
Churchill asked Weitzmann if he could produce 30,000 tons of synthetic acetone so the British could manufacture cordite gun powder. Weitzmann harnessed his genius and energies to the task and produced the synthetic acetone.

"And In Thee Shall All Nations Be Blessed" / 159

When asked what he wanted for his services to England and the free world, he replied, "There is only one thing I want ... a national homeland for my people." On November 2, 1917 the Balfour Declaration was issued which promised the Jews of the world a homeland in Palestine.

The tide of victory or defeat in World War I was in the hands of a Jewish scientist. "In thee shall all the nations of the earth be blessed."

Albert Einstein — WW II

When the Axis powers plunged the world into twelve years of living hell (1933-1945) historically known as World War II, it was again the seed of Abraham to whom God has chosen to reveal the secrets of the universe (Duet 29:29) who provided the knowledge to stop the Axis powers within days.

Albert Einstein (1879-1955), physicist, discoverer of the theory of relativity, and Nobel Prize winner was born in the German town of Ulm. In January 1933, Hitler came to power and Einstein promptly resigned from his position at the Royal Academy of Sciences and never returned to Germany. A deeply religious man, Einstein was convinced that "the less knowledge a scholar possesses, the further he feels from God. But the greater his knowledge, the nearer his approach to God."

During World War II, secret news reached the U.S. physicist that the German uranium project was progressing and that the prospects of the Nazis having a super weapon produced by atomic energy was very possible.

Einstein, when approached by his friend Szilard, signed a letter to President Roosevelt pointing out the feasibility of atomic energy. It was this letter that sparked the Manhattan Project and gave birth to atomic energy. Although Einstein was opposed to the use of the atomic bomb, President Harry Truman, being advised that Japanese military leaders were prepared to fight a conventional war to the last man, decided to use the bomb to save hundreds of thousands of American lives.

The genius that birthed the formula $E=mc^2$ was Jewish. That same atomic energy will be used to defeat the Russian coalition of Arab states that will attack Israel in the near future. The effects of an atomic blast upon the human body are perfectly described by the prophet Zechariah in 13:12;

"And this is the plague with which the Lord will strike all the nations that fought against Jerusalem. Their flesh will rot *while they are still standing* on their feet, their eyes will rot in their sockets, and their tongues will rot in their mouths."

The Automobile

The automobile which has revolutionized life on our planet was not the brain child of Henry Ford. The only invention Henry Ford came up with was the assembly line concept for mass production. The automobile began with the birth of the internal combustion engine which was created by two German Jews named Otto

"And In Thee Shall All Nations Be Blessed" / 161

and Rudolf Diesel. Otto developed the first stage which worked on coal dust and Diesel improved the engine by developing the coal oil injection system.

The relatives of Otto and Diesel, the Daimler family, were in the logging business and were looking for a way to help the horses pull the heavy logs out of the forest. They installed an Otto-Diesel engine on a logging wagon and to their delight discovered the horses were not needed. The auto-truck was born!

Gottlieb Daimler and Benz, an associate of Otto and Diesel, merged and began building the auto-wagons. Mr. Benz had a daughter named Mercedes who wanted a small engine for her buggy which her loving father gladly constructed. The Mercedes Benz was born!

Henry Ford was an anti-Semite who brought to America the fraudulent documents fabricated by the Russian Secret Police under the Czar to justify the Jewish persecutions in Russia. These fraudulent documents were called "The Protocols of the Learned Elders of Zion." This invention of deception and hatred against the Jews was published in a series of articles entitled "The International Jew" by the newspaper "The Dearborn Independent" which was owned by Henry Ford. Henry Ford purged his company of all Jews!

The Telephone

The invention of the telephone was the genius of a German Jew named Phillip Reis in 1860. He and his associate, Greenberg, improved the invention and brought it to America for manufacturing and merchandising. A Jewish financier in Cincinnati named Loth

162 / "And In Thee Shall All Nations Be Blessed"

sent Greenberg to Alexander Graham Bell with his device.

When Bell discovered that Greenberg was ignorant of American patent laws, he filed a patent under his own name. Loth and Greenberg took the case to the Supreme Court in the Loth-Greenberg vs. Bell appeal. The Supreme Court upheld the Loth-Greenberg claim and made Bell pay a token reparation for stealing the device. For many years following, Bell Telephone was anti-Semitic in their employment practices.

The Jewish contribution continued in America through the lives of Supreme Court Justices Felix Frankfurter and Louis Brandeis. Medical journals bulge with the names of Jewish physicians whose medical discoveries have saved tens of thousands of lives. In spite of their small number they have dominated the major fields of human endeavor. Master merchants, humanitarians, scientists, astronauts, statesmen, educators, writers, musicians and gifted entertainers who have blessed our lives a thousand times on dreary days with a God given genius.

How many times have you invited these people into your home through the miracle of celloid or the printed page? Douglas Fairbanks, Cary Grant, Kirk Douglas, Paul Newman, Shelley Winters, James Caan, George Segal, Goldie Hawn, Dustin Hoffman, Peter Sellers, Debra Winger, Lauren Bacall, John Houseman, Madeline Kahn, Barbara Streisand, Danny Kaye, Edward G. Robinson, Tony Curtis, Rod Steiger, Tony Randall, Jack Klugman, Hal Linden, Peter Falk, Ed Asner, Loren Greene, George Burns and Gracie Allen, David

"And In Thee Shall All Nations Be Blessed"

Janssen, Jack Benny, Michael Landon, Linda Lavin, Ted Koppel, Howard Cosell, Barbara Walters, Mike Wallace and Ann Landers to name le creme de le creme. These people are a living testimony; "in thee shall all the nations of the earth be blessed."

From the time of Joseph in Egypt, to Jesus of Nazareth, to Weitzmann in England, to Einstein in America... God has always placed the Jewish people at the major intersections of history to bless the nations.

The late Sam Levenson wrote, "It's a free world. You don't have to like Jews, but if you don't, I suggest that you boycott certain Jewish products like insulin, discovered by Dr. Minkoski; the vaccine for hepatitis discovered by Baruch Blumberg; chlorhydrate for convulsions discovered by Dr. J. Von Liebig; the Wassermann test for syphilis; streptomycin, discovered by Dr. Selman Abraham Waxman; the polio pill by Dr. Albert Sabin; and the polio vaccine by Dr. Jonas Salk.

Good! Boycott! But humanitarianism requires that my people offer all these gifts to all the people of the world. Fanaticism requires that all bigots accept diabetes, hepatitis, convulsions, syphilis, infectious diseases and infantile paralysis.

You want to be mad? Be mad! But I'm telling you, you ain't going to feel so good."

CHAPTER ELEVEN
SHOULD CHRISTIANS SUPPORT ISRAEL?

Support of national Israel does not mean that a person endorses every political action of the government. Support of Israel means the support of Biblical Zionism which is the conviction that God made an eternal and everlasting covenant with Abraham that his seed through Isaac and Jacob would have a Biblical mandate to possess the land of Israel forever.
Should Christians support Israel?

God Did!

God the Father was the first Zionist! As the original land owner, He gave to Abraham, Isaac and Jacob and their descendants the land of Israel forever. Consider the following:

(1) All other nations were created by an act of men, Israel was created by an act of God! (Genesis 12:1-3)

(2) God Himself entered into an elaborate Blood Covenant which was eternal and unconditional with Abraham. In this covenant God gave the Jews a Biblical mandate to possess the land forever. (Genesis 15:8-21)

(3) The boundaries of national Israel were registered in the Word of God. (Genesis 15:18-21 and Ezekiel 47:13 through 48:1-29)

(4) God has personally sworn to protect and defend national Israel. (Psalm 121:4 Ezekiel 38:18-23)

(5) God designed the flag of Israel and promised to gather the Jews back to the land under those colors. (Isaiah 11:12)

(6) Jehovah God promised that Israel would be re-created in a day (Isa. 66:8) That became reality on May 15, 1948 when the United Nations announced the formal recognition of the State of Israel.

(7) God has chosen national Israel and the Jewish people as His own inheritance. (Psalm 33:12)

Is it not logical to state that since God created Israel, and defends Israel, that those who fight with Israel, fight with God!

Jesus Did!

Replacement theologians are teaching that there is not one word in the New Testament that remotely suggest that Christians should support Israel! Wrong! Jesus Christ is our example and He personally taught us by His conduct that Gentiles who support national Israel have His special blessing.

In Luke, chapter seven, Jesus entered Capernaum where a certain Roman Centurion (a Gentile) had a servant that was about to die. When the Centurion heard that Jesus was coming, he sent Jewish elders to Him, pleading for Jesus to come and heal the critically ill servant.

Notice the logic the Jewish elders used with Jesus. They said:

"And when they came to Jesus, they begged Him earnestly, saying that the one (the Centurion) was

Should Christians Support Israel? / 167

worthy, for he *loves our nation (Israel), and has built us a synagogue.* Then Jesus went with them ... "(Luke 7:4-6)

The Scriptural truth is this: Jesus went to the house of this Gentile and healed the servant who was near death because this Gentile had blessed the nation of Israel.

Does it make a difference if Christians bless the nation of Israel? The question must be asked: "Why did God select the house of Cornelius to be the first Gentile house to hear the gospel and to receive the outpouring of the Holy Spirit?" The clear answer is recorded in the book of Acts, chapter ten.

Cornelius was a Roman Centurion, (a Gentile), living in the coastal city of Caesarea who is described in the Scripture as "a devout man and one who feared God ... and who *gave alms generously to the people."* Which people? The Jews who were living in Caesarea whom he controlled through the Roman Army.

The Scripture repeats that the reason God selected the residence of Cornelius for this great spiritual blessing was because he blessed the Jewish people. Verse thirty-one records,

"Cornelius, your prayer has been heard, and *your alms are remembered* in the sight of God." (10:31)

Why was the house of Cornelius selected to receive this great blessing? Because he blessed the Jewish people in the nation of Israel!

Is it really important that Christians bless the national of Israel and the Jewish people? Jehovah God told Abraham that all anti-Semites are under His

168 / Should Christians Support Israel?

curse! (Genesis 12:1-3) Jesus Christ announced that all anti-Semites will come under the judgment of God during the Judgment of the Nations.

Few Christians recognize that there are five judgments in the Scripture. The first is past and four are yet to be. The First Judgment was upon sin at the Cross (Romans 8:1), the Second Judgment will be at the Judgment Seat of Christ where all believers will give an account of the lives they lived on earth before God (2 Corinthians 5:10 and I Corinthians 3:10-15).

The Third Judgment is the Judgment of the Jewish people (Ezekiel 20:34-38, Jeremiah 30:4-7 and Daniel 12:1). The Fourth Judgment is the Judgment of the Nations where the nations of the earth will be judged before God Almighty and His holy angels for the manner in which they treated the Jewish people (Matthew 25:31-46). The Fifth Judgment is the Great White Throne Judgment for the wicked dead who are released from hell to appear before God for formal sentencing before they are cast into the Lake of Fire forever (Revelation 20:11-15).

Back to the Fourth Judgment! The time of this judgment is immediately after the Messiah returns to earth to establish His literal kingdom in the city of Jerusalem. It is critical to your well being that you understand what the Bible teaches, not what Replacement theologians are saying.

Who are these hungry, naked, thirsty, sick, imprisoned strangers of Matthew, chapter twenty five?

Should Christians Support Israel? / 169

They are the Jewish people of history, not the church. Jesus clarifies this with;
"And the King will answer and say unto them, 'Assuredly, I say unto you, inasmuch as you did it unto the *least of these my brethren,* (the Jews), you did it unto me. Then He will also say to those on the left hand, 'Depart from me, you cursed, into everlasting fire prepared for the devil and his angels.' And these shall go away into everlasting punishment, but the righteous into eternal life" (Matthew 25:40-41 & 46).

Is it important to be right on the Israel question? When you consider that being wrong brings you under the curse of God and headed for eternal, everlasting fire with the devil and his angels... it's important! Israel is not a "take it or leave it" subject. It is a life and death matter... eternal life!

Paul Did!

The Apostle Paul did! He records the relationship Gentiles are to have with the Jewish people in Romans 15:27:

" ... For if the Gentiles have been partakers of their spiritual things, *their duty* is to minister to them in material things."

Will You Support Israel?

If you believe the Bible to be the inspired Word of God and those who reject its truths have entered into idolatry and rebellion, if you believe that Jehovah God is a God of covenant whose integrity would make it impossible for Him to break covenant, if you believe that Jesus Christ is our example and that we are to follow Him, there is no Biblical alternative but to be supportive of the nation of Israel and the Jewish people.

Footnotes—Chapter One

1. Dawidowicz, Lucy S., "The War Against the Jews 1933-1945" Bantam Books, 1975, pg. 27.
2. Runes, Dagobert D., "The War Against the Jew," Philosophical Library, New York, 1968, pg. 114.
3. Dawidowicz, Lucy S., "The War Against the Jews 1933-1945," Bantam Books, 1975, pg. 29.
4. Kaplan, Gil, "Israel's History of Persecution," pg. 23.
5. Flannery, Edward H., "The Anguish of the Jews," Paulist Press, 1985, pg. 51.
6. Hay, Malcomb, "The Roots of Christian Anti-Semitism," Freedom Liberty Press, New York City, pg. 37.
7. Runes, Dagobert D., "The War Against the Jew," Philosophical Library, New York, 1968, pg. 34.
8. Encyclopedia Judaica, Keter Publishing House, Jerusalem, 1978, Vol. 10, pg. 1446 and Vol. 4, pg. 64.
9. Kisch, "Jews in Medieval Germany," pg. 203.
10. Runes, Dagobert D., "The War Against the Jew," Philosophical Library, New York, 1968, pg. 87.
11. Hay, Malcomb, "The Roots of Christian Anti-Semitism," Freedom Liberty Press, New York City, pg. 160.
12. Ibid, pg. 167.
13. Ibid, pg. 167.
14. Encyclopedia Judaica, Keter Publishing House, Jerusalem, 1978, Vol. 3, pg. 103.
15. Hay, Malcomb, "The Roots of Christian Anti-Semitism," Freedom Liberty Press, New York City, pg. 169.
16. Runes, Dagobert D., "The War Against the Jew," Philosophical Library, New York, 1968, pg. 114.
17. Hay, Malcomb, "The Roots of Christian Anti-Semitism," Freedom Library Press, New York City, pg. 11.
18. Ibid, pg. 12.
19. Ibid, pg. 3
20. Toland, John, "Adolf Hitler," Doubleday & Company, Inc., Garden City, New York, 1978, Vol. 1, pg. 326.
21. Toland, John, "Adolf Hitler," Doubleday & Company, Inc., Garden City, New York, 1978, Vol. 2, pg. 803.

22. Toland, John "Adolf Hitler," Doubleday & Company, Inc., Garden City, New York, Vol. 1, pg. 331.
23. Toland, John, "Adolf Hitler," Doubleday & Company, Inc., Garden City, Vol. 2, pg. 617.
24. Toland, John, "Adolf Hitler," Doubleday & Company, Inc., Garden City, New York, Vol. 1, pg. 481.
25. Toland, John, "Adolf Hitler," Doubleday & Company, Inc., Garden City, New York, Vol. 2, pg. 687.
26. Toland, John, "Hitler, the Pictorial Documentary of His Life," Doubleday & Company, Inc., Garden City, New York, pg. 287.
27. Toland, John, "Adolf Hitler," Doubleday & Company, Garden City, New York, Vol. 1, pg. 233.
28. Dawidowicz, Lucy S., "The War Against the Jews 1933-1945," Bantam Books, 1975, pg. 25.
29. Toland, John, "Adolf Hitler," Doubleday & Company, Inc., Garden City, New York, 1978, Vol. 2, pg. 593.
30. Paulk, Earl, "To Whom Is God Betrothed?" K Dimension Publishers, Atlanta, Georgia, 1985, pg. 43.

Footnotes—Chapter Two
1. Hay, Malcomb, "The Roots of Christian Anti-Semitism," Freedom Library Press, New York City, pg. 20.
2. Ibid, pg 20.
3. Potok, Chaim, "Wanderings," Fawcett Crest, New York, pg. 263.
4. Ibid, pg. 265.
5. See Finis Jennings Dake's footnote "e" from Mark 10 and footnote "m" from St. Matthew 19. Dake's Annotated Reference Bible, Atlanta, Georgia.
6. Jones, Vendyl, "Will the Real Jesus Please Stand?" Institute of Judaic-Christian Research, Tyler, Texas, pg. 7-25.

Footnotes—Chapter Three
1. Hay, Malcomb, "The Roots of Christian Anti-Semitism," Freedom Library Press, New York 1981, pg. 24.
2. Ibid, pg. 26.

3. Runes, Dagobert R., "The War Against the Jews," Philosophical Library, Inc., New York, pg. 42.
4. Hay, Malcomb, "The Roots of Christian Anti-Semitism," Freedom Library Press, New York, 1981, pg. 8.
5. Ibid, pg. 9.
6. Ibid, pg. 11.

Footnotes—Chapter Four

1. Paulk, Earl, "To Whom is God Betrothed?" K-Dimension Publishers, Atlanta, Georgia 1985, pg. 40.

Footnotes—Chapter Five

1. Paulk, Earl, "To Whom is God Betrothed?" K. Dimension Publishers, Atlanta, Georgia 1985 pg. 47.

Footnotes—Chapter Seven

1. Paulk, Earl, "To Whom is God Betrothed?" K. Dimension Publishers, Atlanta Georgia 1985 pg. 3.
2. Jones, Vendyl, "Will the Real Jesus Please Stand" Institute of Judaic-Christian Research, Tyler, Texas pg. 2-31.

ABOUT THE AUTHOR

Pastor John C. Hagee is the senior pastor of Cornerstone Church, a non-denominational, evangelical, church located in San Antonio, Texas. Cornerstone Church has a staff of forty-five and a thriving membership that presently exceeds 2800 families.

Pastor Hagee was born April 12, 1940 in Baytown, Texas, the second of four sons to Rev. & Mrs. B. Hagee. He is married to Diana Castro Hagee and they are blessed with five children, Letisha, Christopher, Christina, Matthew and Sandy.

Educational background includes the public schools of Houston, Texas where he graduated as the Valedictorian of his class and was a multi-sport letterman. He attended Trinity University of San Antonio on a football scholarship and was on the Academic Dean's List graduating in 1964 with a B.S. Degree. He also attended North Texas State University where he received his Master's Degree in 1966. His theological training came at Southwestern Assemblies of God College in Waxahachie where he was President of his class and sang in the Harvester Choir.

Pastor Hagee was awarded the "Humanitarian of the Year" Award by the San Antonio B'nai B'rith Council. This was the first time that this award has been given to a Gentile. He was honored with the Henrietta Szold Award by the Texas Southern Region of Hadassah. He was honored by the San Antonio Chapter of Hadassah as a Founder for the Hadassah Hospital in Jerusalem in 1981, 1982 and 1983. He is the founder and Executive Director of "A Night to Honor Israel!"

About the Author

He was presented the ZOA Israel Service Award by the Zionist Organization in Dallas on November 12, 1983, which was presented the following year to U.N. Ambassador Jean Kirkpatrick. Pastor Hagee was presented the ZOA Service Award in Houston on November 17, 1984 which was given the following year to Gov. Mark White of Texas. Mayor Kathy Whitmire issued a special proclamation in his honor declaring November 17, 1984 as "PASTOR JOHN C. HAGEE DAY" in Houston.

Pastor Hagee is also the President and Chairman of the Board of Global Evangelism Television and can be seen on television nationally over the TBN network. He is the author of several books.

DOMINION PUBLICATIONS BY JOHN HAGEE

ORDER FORM

Please send me the following items: Qty.   Amount

BOOKS: (Requested donation $7.00 each)

_____	Should Christians Support Israel?	_____	$_____
_____	The Genesis Curse	_____	$_____
_____	Invasion of Demons	_____	$_____
_____	Like a Cleansing Fire	_____	$_____
_____	The Scandalous Saint	_____	$_____
_____	Why We Support Israel ($2.00)	_____	$_____

CASSETTE TAPE SERIES

_____ OUR JEWISH ROOTS (8 tapes) This series explores the Israeli-Arab dispute, the Genesis Curse, Church Procedure that became Hitler's Policy and Our Jewish Roots. Cost: $40.00 $_____

_____ IS THERE A FAMILY IN YOUR HOUSE? (5 tapes) God is the architect of the family. Hear "God's Plan for the Father/Husband, God's Plan for the Mother/Wife, God's Plan for the Children, God's Plan for Singles." Cost: $25.00 $_____

_____ THE EIGHT NAMES OF GOD (12 tapes) What does it mean when we say, "Our Father which art in heaven, *hallowed be thy name?*" God will do what His name implies. Twelve tapes that shook a congregation of thousands into a deeper spiritual walk with God. Cost: $49.95 $_____

_____ PROPHECY SERIES (9 tapes) A Biblical exploration of the future! The next event in God's prophetic program! The Church and the Tribulation. God's Picture of the Tribulation. Israel's Title Deed to the Land, Daniel's Image, The Coming Anti-Christ, The Great Harlot and the Battle of Armageddon. Cost: $45.00 $_____

_____ WHAT IS A GREAT CHURCH? (2 tapes) A tape series every church member in America should hear describing God's portrait of a great church. Cost: $10.00 $_____

_____ COMMUNICATION IN MARRIAGE (2 tapes) You can talk without communicating! Learn that there are five levels of communication and that few married couples truly communicate. Cost: $10.00 $_____

CASSETTE TAPE SINGLES (Each tape $5.00)

		Qty.	Amount
_____	The Terminal Generation (Ten Bible reasons why this could be the generation that will see the Rapture of the Church)	_____	$ _____
_____	"Blessed is the Man ..."	_____	$ _____
_____	The Pursuit of Excellence	_____	$ _____
_____	Flee From Idolatry (an expose of idolatry that exists in every church in America.)	_____	$ _____
_____	Why We Honor the Jews!	_____	$ _____
_____	Take A Stand!	_____	$ _____
_____	Get Mad!	_____	$ _____
_____	Steps Toward Unity!	_____	$ _____
_____	Endure to the End!	_____	$ _____
_____	A Sound Mind	_____	$ _____
_____	How Free is Freedom?	_____	$ _____
_____	Should Christians be in Politics?	_____	$ _____
_____	Stand Up to Life!	_____	$ _____

TOTAL FOR ORDER $ _____

Please allow four to six weeks for delivery. If quicker delivery is desired, add 15% to the cost of your total order for FIRST-CLASS POSTAGE AND HANDLING (For U.S. residents only)................................... $ _____

For residents outside the U.S.A. add 6% for postage... $ _____

TOTAL AMOUNT ENCLOSED $ _____

Name _____

Address _____

City _____ State _____ Zip _____

Telephone ( ) _____

Just in case there is a question concerning your order.
For a complete tape catalogue of John Hagee tapes write to:

John Hagee Ministries
P.O. Box 691265
San Antonio, Texas 78269